A Way Out:

A Story of Race, Poverty & Christianity

Angela Fields

Beyond Love Publishing

New Jersey

ISBN: 9780982777442 Paperback

Library of Congress Control Number: 2021911360

Book Cover Design by Kailin Jones

Printed in the United States of America.

First printing edition 2021.

Beyondlovepublishing.com

Email: info@beyondlovepublishing.com

This book is dedicated to my parents

whose hardships and toil were not in vain.

To my Dad

who knew God's calling for

my life before I did.

To my Mom

who is my cornerstone.

A Foreword to A Way Out by Angela Fields

Dr. Stephen Hahn

❧

I am pleased to be asked by Angela Fields to provide a foreword to her book *A Way Out: A Story of Race, Poverty, and Christianity* because it represents to me an act of faith extended across what otherwise might be thought of as difference become division.

We are both people created in the image of God; and mundanely enough one of us is Black and the other is white; one female, one male. We are both people of faith; one of us by an explicit commission and ordination and the other by participating in a once "mainstream" religious tradition, in which some might find not so much a divide as a difference in spirit. When we met some years ago, I was in a position of power and privilege in a very busy Office of the Provost at the university where Reverend Fields, then simply Angela, was a student and, moreover, a student worker in the front end of the same office. I did not know Angela well, but I would see her several times a week as I came in to or left the office and we would smile and say "Hello!" Her smile was genuine and I appreciated that. There was a point when Angela was not there and I believe I asked why that was so and found that there was some kind of problem, but my respondents were vague about what it was. Then Angela was there again, day to day, and she soon graduated.

It was some years later that I met Angela again at a breakfast meeting for people in a leadership alliance of non-profit organizations in Paterson, NJ. Her smile was again genuine, and we renewed our acquaintance. By this time Angela had become Reverend Angela Fields and she held a senior position in a well-established and critically important non-profit social service agency that had been founded by a member of a religious order. As we caught up on intervening history, Reverend Fields told me that she was interested in writing a book organized around nine or ten things that she wished someone had told her as a young woman embarking on a path toward ministry. I told her I would be glad to read it if she wanted informal feedback, and she thanked me for my interest.

Later she did contact me about reading the manuscript and commenting on it, which I was glad to do. The truth is I learned a great deal from the perspective and point of view of the narrator of the book—and this is something different from what is often possible talking person-to-person.

By way of introducing the book I can say that it strikes me as an honest, wise, and humorous profession of her calling, grounded in faith, and valuable not only as a book of advice to readers who may be interested in pursuing an explicit calling to ministry. It is, in addition, a testimony and witness to a Christian critique of race, social inequity, and poverty in the United States as persistent causes of despair and engines of a self-perpetuating cycle of degradation to the detriment of all. Her experience as it unfolds in the telling of her particular "story" is an important element in the proof of what she holds to be true: God loves you.

God loves you, therefore...

Her story begins with a comparison of her contemporary situation and calling with the biblical story of Moses, and I'll leave it at that for her telling. I will say that is a story grounded in the Christian tradition that we share, in an analysis of inequity it is based upon faith in that tradition and scripture; and that is not simply oriented toward conventional notions of assent to doctrine, but toward action and application in the lives of people. God loves you, therefore....

The form of the chapters is sermonic—each chapter brings together something from the Bible, something from personal experience and something from collective wisdom to enlighten and encourage the hearer or reader in faith. (Central to these chapters are the story of Moses in Exodus; Peter's vision in the Acts of the Apostles that God does not discriminate between peoples based on status or nationality or race; the Sermon on the Plain and Jesus' admonition to love one another; and Paul's petition to his listeners in I Corinthians to consider how they are called and to recollect the inspiration of Isaiah regarding the worldly wisdom of privilege.) The biblical basis is a framework for thinking through experience, guided as well by social science and the wisdom of leaders in faith such as Martin Luther King, Howard Thurman, the nineteenth century English preacher Charles Spurgeon and others. A good bit of humor, self-revelation, humility, and insight enriches the reader's experience.

God loves you, therefore you have the opportunity and obligation to try to get it right, to fail and to ask forgiveness, sincerely, and in the words of the prophet Micah "to do justice and to love kindness and to walk humbly with your God" (Micah 6:8; NRSV) not as dejected acts of penance or trivial acts of social acceptance but as something real. To do justice and love kindness, together. Imagine. That is, at least in part, the message imparted here which is made more vivid by being embedded in an honest and compelling story. An important message, now as then. It is the point of the story, the argument, of Psalm 139.

The original intent to illustrate some stumbling blocks and blind spots that Reverend Fields encountered on her journey is realized here for people singularly called to ordained Christian ministry, but the insights of the book are there for all who feel the inkling or the strong pulse of a calling to serve God and others in their everyday lives, or even to do right in the habits of daily life.

This is a story of convictions deeply felt and convincingly expressed. I am honored to convey my appreciation for being asked to commend this book to you. I hope you find it a blessing conferred.

Preface: Exodus

꘏

This book was quite a feat, but it came together amazingly. I was nervous about writing about such complex topics related to race, poverty, and Christianity. Each topic has affected me in such profound ways – some personally and some professionally. However, it is not my will but yours, God.

My dad, Cyres is now with the Lord. This book is dedicated to his memory.

I remember calling my dad, Cyres, and telling him the stories I am about to tell you in this book. My dad told me to write this book. His exact statement was "Give America a mirror. Sometimes people just need to see themselves."

> For if anyone is a hearer of the word and not a doer, he is like a man who looks at his natural face in a mirror; for once he has looked at himself and gone away, he has immediately forgotten what kind of person he was. But one who looks intently at the perfect law, the law of liberty, and abides by it, not having become a forgetful hearer but an effectual doer, this man will be blessed in what he does. (James 1:23-25 NASB)

Therefore, the "why" of this book is as follows. First, I want America to reflect on multiple generations of race, poverty, and

Christianity broadly and personally. I will be weaving together research and my personal testimony throughout the book. Most are familiar with the structural and individual barriers the "disinherited" face in society that overwhelming affects the poor and BIPOC. However, I do not hear enough mainstream Christian voices denouncing the dehumanization of people groups in the name of the Almighty.

Second, I want to highlight how mainstream Christianity's silence propels race and poverty issues. Third, I want to encourage and empower people like me who live under the weight of it all. Your way out may not look like your counterparts', but it is possible. It will be filled with ups and downs – struggles and triumphs, famine and abundance. But you can do it. And when you find your way out, lead others out. Lastly, if we are who we believe we are as Christians and as a nation, we will do the internal and external work to resemble the redeeming nature of Christ.

A little background on me. I knew my calling early. I am called to be a conduit of Christ in the community. However, knowing my calling and walking in it were two different things. Therefore, I am drawn to God's servant leader Moses in the Bible. I am especially interested in Moses' assignment to go back to Egypt and free the Israelites. God commissioned Moses to go back to Egypt to fight for the people – with the people. However, Moses fled Egypt and escaped persecution forty years earlier for a "righteous" kill. So, when God commanded Moses to go back to a place of danger sometime later, he was apprehensive. Now, I am non-violent, but I understand it is hard going back to a place you fled.

Racism or an oppressive system is not an easy thing to challenge. It is rather exhausting. I understand Moses' perspective when he says, "Please send someone else!" How often do we want God to send someone else?

Moses, like many of us, did not realize the person he had become while in Midian. Midian was the training ground for Moses' assignment. In Midian, Moses was shepherding for forty years. Moses' assignment was not only about freeing the people but leading the people.

When God revealed a portion of the vision for my life to me, I cried. I told **God** that the vision was too big for me. Unbelievable right? I did not know the woman I would become and am becoming.

Once, Moses had successfully led the people out of Egypt and The Lord was giving Moses instruction for the next phase of the journey. The Lord, however, is angry with the stubbornness of the people. Therefore, the Lord tells Moses that His presence will not accompany them on the journey. Moses, then, meets with God face-to face at the Tent of Meeting. I love the imagery of talking to God one -to- one as a friend.

Moses says, "You have been telling me, 'Lead these people,' but you have not let me know whom you will send with me. You have said, 'I know you by name and you have found favor with me.'…Remember that this nation is your people." The Lord replied, "My Presence will go with you, and I will give you rest."

Then Moses said to him, "If your Presence does not go with us, do not send us up from here. And the Lord said to Moses, "I will do the very thing you have asked, because I am pleased with you and I know you by name." (Exodus 33:12-17 NIV)

All of my life, I was waiting for someone to go with me as well. All my dreams and goals were contingent on my sister or someone else doing it with me. I believed I could not do it by myself. My prayer for a long time was "God bring someone to help me *do this*". Whatever it was. However, I always went alone.

It was years later when I discovered my meaning behind bring someone with me. I needed someone to "hide" behind when I needed to withdraw mentally, spiritually, emotionally, and physically.

But I now know that God had multiple people journeying with me. I just had to change my mind set. I have an amazing support system. They are not called to travel with me, but they are there when I need them to laugh, cry, support and celebrate me and vice versa. Like Moses, I had been asking for something God already answered. Although, I travel alone, people are making the trip with me. Moses did not realize his someone – Joshua – was traveling with him.

How many of us are praying for things God already answered but we just cannot see it?

In all our small mindedness...our thoughts and ways are so limited. But Moses knew the most important thing. God had to be present for him to prosper.

The Lord, too, is my portion.

Let us pursue the mission of God together. This book is about overcoming obstacles whether they are internal or external that hinder our pursuit in life. In many ways we are all a lost and wandering people, pushed, and pulled by the internal and external circumstances of life.

My life experiences are not just for me. They are to help others.

- Selah

Acknowledgement

I would like to thank God for this amazing journey of putting together a book that was so life-giving and therapeutic through the darkest of times. I would again like to thank my earthly father for speaking over me and believing in my abilities before I did. I would like to thank my mom for always being there for me. I love you so much lady. You are my Daisy and I am your sunflower for life and beyond. I would also like to give a very special thank you to Dr. Stephen Hahn. Dr. Hahn is Professor Emeritus of English at William Paterson University. Thank you so much for giving me your time and talents selflessly. Thanks for being available for me to talk through the hard parts of the book and authentically hearing my struggles. You were there to encourage me, challenge me, and help me not shy away from scripture. Your words reminded me of Pastor Gwen Brown's teaching that the power lays in the Word of God.

I would also like to acknowledge Beth Perry, Dr. D. Gushee, Dr. P. Durso, Renee Koubiadis and Tanisha Dixon for your preliminary review and feedback. Thank you to everyone who have ever supported my ministry of writing. You all have made me stronger.

God bless you!

Contents

A Foreword to A Way Out by Angela Fields v

Preface: Exodus ix

Acknowledgement xiv

Chapter 1: Let my People Go 1

Chapter 2: Poverty: Roots and Realities 11

Chapter 3 : The Masterplan vs. the Master's Plan.................27

Chapter 4: Validation 53

Chapter 5: Fifty Shades of Race: I'm Perfectly Different 67

Chapter 6: No invitation, no thank you...........................81

Chapter 7 : Taking the lead................................93

Chapter 8: We are all connected 107

Chapter 9: Finish the Race: We Shall Overcome..............119

Footnotes by Chapter...130

Bibliography 140

Chapter 1

Let my People Go

Then the Lord said to Moses, "Go to Pharaoh and say to him, This is what the Lord says: Let my people go, so that they may worship me."

Exodus 8:1

"Never underestimate the power of your own story," my Christian Ethics professor once said. This is my truth.

My mom and dad, Daisy and Cyres were born in South Carolina in the mid-40's. They received an elementary school education in South Carolina. The quality of a fourth and sixth grade education for African Americans in the South in the 1950s was limited at best. Children went to school between one to three half-days per week. The rest of the week were spent helping their families in the fields or at home. All things being equal, an elementary school education could not come close to preparing a person to face life's challenges. I often ask myself,

"What if my mom and dad had equal educational opportunities in life?" "What did I learn in the fourth grade?" "How could a sixth-grade education propel someone into the world with the knowledge to build an adequate life or raise a family?" I cannot imagine facing the world, let alone providing for a family, with a fourth or sixth grade education. But I think that is the point.

My mother explained that there were a few families living on the sharecropper's land. These families were responsible for all aspects of farming the land. Extra people were only brought in during cotton season. My granddad never obtained a driver's license as he drove a horse and buggy from the sharecropper's farm. Money was scarce as you could imagine. My mom's family did not have the things that we take for granted. For instance, my grandfather made the mattresses and pillows, for his family of seven, by stuffing 'Lowcountry Spanish Moss' – a bromeliad plant – in between fabric and sewing it up. When he was able, he would put bird feathers in the mattress as well.

My spirit rejoices in this moment because I want to proudly proclaim that I have come from a long line of people who responded to life's challenges – slavery, plantation life, sharecropping, low educational attainment – and remained resilient.

When the sharecropping era was over, my mom could only obtain incredibly low paying jobs working with live chickens at the chicken house or hurling watermelons onto the truck. My dad found work at the local lumberyard. My father was a spiritual man. One day, he had an epiphany while working in the woods sawing limbs off a tree for the lumberyard. Cyres envisioned greater opportunities for himself and his growing family. My father gathered his wife and three children and fled from the South to the Northeast seeking the better opportunities he envisioned. My parents found a way out.

In New Jersey, my parents faced huge obstacles. Apparently, as the pressure increased, so did the lovemaking. Eleven years and ten children after their arrival, my parents were finally able to purchase a home. I was conceived after my family moved into their new home. My conception bloomed out of joy, celebration, and triumph, because my family had moved from tilling the land to becoming landowners. Cyres and Daisy created three additional bundles of joy, totaling fourteen children.

As a child, my bedtime stories were tales from the field. My mother made sure I knew and understood everything that happened before I was born. Her objective was to teach me – "Do not take anything for granted." I remember my mother telling my siblings and me stories of how she hoed and picked cotton in the field with my grandfather. She told us how the cotton pricked and burned the tips of her fingers, leaving them raw to the touch. Raw fingers, however, were not enough to escape a day's work.

She also pulled weeds out of the soybean field and broke corn in the cornfield in season. My dad could attest to the same backbreaking work. Furthermore, I was told that my family inherited our ancestral last name from a Fields plantation – like many others, I am sure. I learned early in life that the stark southern racism and poverty felt by my parents would, naturally, affect my life. Although my parents moved out of the backbreaking, sharing cropping South, their children did not immediately receive the benefits my father envisioned.

Despite my parents' success in becoming property owners, the location of their property became problematic. The neighborhood was experiencing white flight as Paterson, New Jersey was changing. My community began to decline.

I attended the neighborhood public schools that were rocked by poverty, premature sexual encounters, teenage pregnancies, drugs, and violence.

Outside of school, my parents kept us busy. We attended the Boys and Girls Club and joined A.W.A.N.A at Bible Baptist Church. A.W.A.N.A stands for "approved workmen are not ashamed" after 2 Timothy 2:15. If we were old enough to work, we were required to get a job. There was no hanging in the streets.

My saving grace was Bible Baptist Church. Bible Baptist Church was in an affluent suburb in Northern New Jersey. Youth ministers ventured into the vulnerable neighborhoods to reach children in a community stricken by economic woes. They understood that giving clothes and food to families in need was just a starting point. The youth ministry team at Bible Baptist Church embraced me with authentic love. I was invited to church leaders' homes for dinner and was integrated into the lives of the church members. I participated in worship and can still remember my line from the Christmas play where I played an angel: "Behold I bring you good tidings of great joy, which shall be to all people" (Luke 2:10, KJV). I recall the line so well because it was the first time, I felt proud of myself. The youth ministers infused hope into me and revived my spirit. Their collective faith led me to embrace: "I can do everything through Christ, who gives me strength." (Philippians 4:13, NLT)

One Sunday morning, I felt a tugging from the Lord – the Consecration. The Consecration refers to being set apart for a sacred task to answer the call of God. I hung on every word delivered from the pulpit. After service, I ran up to the Pastor and asked him about God's leading. I asked him, "What is it like to be a Christian and do God's work?" He smiled and said with his wide blue eyes staring at me, "Well, Angel, being a dedicated Christian is hard work but whatever the Lord requires us to do - we must do." I felt a gleam in my heart and people noticed it.

Through Bible Baptist Church, I was also able to see outside of my community. This hope and vision of a different future pushed me forward and still propels me onward.

My parents also took the family on fishing outings, picnics, hiking in the mountains, bike riding and other outdoor activities. Cyres and Daisy believed they were strict about receiving an education. Each child was required to earn at least a high school diploma. Receiving a high school diploma was huge to people who had not been allowed to finish primary or middle school.

I took it a step further and became the first child in my family to obtain a bachelor's degree. If I am honest, I did not aspire to continue my education. I went through the motions when I was accepted into William Paterson University. I had no plans of attending. However, I was dating someone at the time, and he went off to college. One day, my boyfriend and I were on the phone and he told me I was stupid. He continued to say that I was not going to be anything, and he was making something out of himself. My biggest motivator is for someone to count me out – a trait I inherited from my mother. In any event, he attended my graduation from William Paterson University before he attended his own graduation.

My first professional position out of college was within a non-profit organization that specialized in maternal and child health. Stress is one of the leading causes of pre-term labor. Pre-term labor can lead to a host of health problems for mom and child. My role was helping women tackle the source of their stress to ensure a healthy full-term baby. I was so eager to get started in the position and meet the women. I wrote out my speaking points for the mothers and mothers-to-be about caring for both themselves and their babies. On my first day out of training, I packed my Samsonite rolling briefcase. I made sure it was equipped with everything I needed for mother and baby. Motherhood pamphlets…check; relaxation techniques…check; "Sound of Nature" sound boxes to accompany relaxation techniques… check. I was ready.

Early the next morning, I arrived at the neighborhood federally qualified health center (FQHC) and arranged my goodies on the table. As the first pregnant mom waded into my office, I greeted her excitedly and offered her a seat. After a few preliminary questions I asked the mom, "So what are your stressors?" The mom replied, "I am a prostitute. I have five children in foster care, and I am pregnant with twins. I want to get out of this life, but my boyfriend is my pimp. He is waiting for me outside. Can you help me?"

I did not have a pamphlet for that.

I scheduled the mom-to-be for a one-on-one session with a licensed counselor to help her work through her "stressors."

The same day I met a young lady who was nineteen years old and six months pregnant. She had come to the health center for her *first* prenatal care appointment. The young lady was informed that she was HIV positive and due to the lack of the preventative measures, her baby would be as well. The young woman asked, "What do I do now?"

I did not have a relaxation technique or therapeutic sound for that either.

For months, I listened to mothers and mothers-to-be share life-altering stories of suffering within communities near me. Women who were pregnant and homeless with incarcerated partners. Pregnant women using substances as a means of coping with stressors. Pregnant women employed at stressful places of employment. There was a crisis in the community and children were being ensnared in the crumbling. Children were going into the foster care system. Babies were being born extremely underweight with a host of health problems. Minority children are most affected by pre-term labor and health disparities. I wanted to do more for the mothers, but my hands were tied as I was confined to the guidelines of the initiative.

I began to pray for the afflictions of the women and children within the community. I meditated on the following verses from Philippians: "Therefore if you have any encouragement from being united with Christ, if any comfort from his love, if any common sharing in the Spirit, if any tenderness and compassion, then make my joy complete by being like-minded, having the same love, being one in spirit and of one mind. Do nothing out of selfish ambition or vain conceit. Rather, in humility value others above yourselves." (Philippians 2:1-3 NIV)

I asked God to help the people who are hurting in the community. The more I prayed for God to help the community, the deeper my spirit wrestled with the neglect within communities. I did not know that God was sending me to help the people in the community.

Through prayer and the guidance of the Spirit, I traded in my professional position for a deeper spiritual position. At midnight in December of 2006, I was awakened and given instructions out of nowhere. It was crystal clear, and I knew God was moving me to my appointed place to begin training me for my work in the community. I could feel the call, the spiritual unrest. He knew the plans for me, plans to prosper and not harm me; the plans to give me hope and a future. Confused, with plenty of questions and even more tears, I surrendered to his will.

My push toward higher education and my introduction

into the community was a set up for God's continued plan for my life. We who have chosen to follow Jesus are in a line of faithful people who challenged the way things are and dare to believe change is possible. Now, some of you may look at yourself as I looked at myself.

To be honest...I cried. I had no idea how God was going to use me. How I could challenge anyone? The best answer I ever received from a ministry leader to the question of how is YES. She did not even let me ask the full question. She just said, "The answer to how is yes." That was good enough for me. I understood that I did not have to know exactly what to do. Also, there is not one way to serve the community. I just had to be open and willing.

But what is community?

This thing called community is not singular. Community is a series of complex and complicated puzzles. There is a strong sense of struggle and hopelessness in communities located on the other side of privilege. Privilege meaning advantage, advancement, and freedom or exemption from rules and penalty. Circumstances are rarely linear and often begin years prior to our awareness of them. Children are the most affected population.

I began by engaging in the Ministry of Standing with the community. My ministry was divided into four parts, which is *to stand, to stand for, to stand with and to stand up for*. *To stand* simply refers to being moved beyond the point of passive listening and deciding that watching a community suffer needlessly is something I could no longer do. *To stand for* is no longer waiting for someone else to act but to make the decision to help rebuild the community one person at a time. *To stand with* is taking up the cause of the people as a friend, companion, and fellow citizen. Finally, *to stand up for* is to stand up for righteousness, justice, and truth to deter further oppression or suppression of a community. The empowerment of His Spirit gives me the courage to confront the challenges which plague and paralyze the community.

While there are frightening stories of fragmentation, decay, and greed, there are also stories of hope, transformation, and perseverance. Continued hope is the first way out. Hope is so powerful and creates a space for people to dream outside the realm of what they see. Hope drives the imagery of one's future looking different from their past. The grace of God renews the capacity to hope every day creating optimism and rejuvenation of the mind toward new opportunities and outcomes. Hope is momentum enough to propel me forward.

Chapter 2

Poverty: Roots and Realities

*"Because the poor are plundered and the needy groan, I
will now arise," says the Lord. "I will protect them from
those who malign them."*

Psalm 12:5 NIV

Answering the call to community led to deeper levels
of poverty. I knew I had to separate myself from the
community that I was familiar with to gain a comprehensive
understanding of the issues. I left my job in New Jersey and
moved to South Carolina on a whim and signed up for non-
matriculated classes at the University of South Carolina. I was
trying to decide which degree would work best for community
work – MPA, MPH or MBA.

Hmmm...did I mention a young man helped to influence
my decision to go to South Carolina? Listen, do not judge me.
I am not going to pretend it was an easy, no brainer decision to

uproot my life. I was young and looking for love like everyone else. I happened to also be attached to a calling at the same time. Before your mind begins to wander, the courtship ended soon after I arrived in South Carolina. God simply worked through that young man to get me where I needed to be. Ironically, I was back in my parents' home state standing in the place my parents fled. The Lord is more comical than Dave Chapelle.

In August of 2007, I arrived at a motel in Cayce, South Carolina with $200 in the bank. I was economically poor and homeless. I thought that God would connect me with a job and apartment right away. Instantaneous God because I am here to serve you. Things did not happen quite so instantaneously. I spent a week and a half in this smelly motel. A group of men were drinking and tossing beer bottles off the balcony every night. I was so naïve, but I refused to show fear.

I drove to the nearby unemployment office to conduct an employment search and meet with an employment counselor. I guess I was too honest about my situation. I blurted out, "I am staying in a dreadful motel; I do not know anyone. I just moved here with little resources and I need to find a job fast." He looked sympathetic; then he propositioned me for sex. He offered me shelter, "companionship," and an allowance. This man, over thirty years my senior, wanted to be my full-time job. My vulnerability was viewed as an opportunity to take advantage of me. I declined and pushed away from his desk.

I started to have second thoughts about the move. Just then, a woman met me at the door as I was leaving the office. She said, "I see God in your eyes." That was enough to give me hope. I knew God was with me. My intentions for moving to South Carolina were innocent, but I was guilty of failing to plan.

My "failure to plan" is known as "causing your own homelessness" in the social services world. Therefore, you are disqualified from receiving any help. With few resources, I did what any self-respecting adult would do in this situation. I called my mother.

I asked my mother to call an aunt who I did not know very well in Allendale, South Carolina. My mother called and I was off to spend the weekend with my Aunt Daisy. I drove for what seemed like forever to meet Aunt Daisy and Uncle Herbert. It was so strange being there. It was like wearing brand new shoes for the first time. I kept looking down at my feet and wiggling my toes.

We conversed for about an hour, but exhaustion set in. I asked if I could take a nap. Hours later, I woke up to converse further with my newfound relatives. My aunt and uncle sat me down and told me I was not returning to the motel. My Aunt Daisy called her children while I slept. She conferred with them about having me as a house guest. My uncle told me I had a home until I figured things out or one year, whichever came first. That was God's provision to my calling. I went from near homelessness to fully sheltered living with family I had yet to know in Allendale, South Carolina. Now, Allendale County is one of the poorest counties in South Carolina. I learned a great deal about poverty related issues while living and working in Allendale. I was constantly confronted by the damage of low socioeconomic attainment and disinvestment in Allendale.

Poverty in the Community

As a host of commentators tell us, poverty is a multi-faceted phenomenon, which can be measured by various socioeconomic conditions, such as employment, health, education, transportation, and housing.[1] Without adequate transportation, jobs, medical care, schooling, and housing, people cannot gain the access needed to improve their social class: "Poverty is not just a lack of money; it is not having the capability to realize one's full potential as a human being."[2] Poverty is a denial of choices and opportunities, a violation of human dignity. It means a lack of basic capacity to participate effectively in society. It means not having enough to feed and clothe a family, not having a school or clinic to go to, and not having access to credit. It means insecurity, powerlessness and exclusion of individuals, households, and communities. It also means susceptibility to violence, and often implies living on marginal or fragile environments, without access to clean water or sanitation. [3]

"The constraints produced by low incomes are exacerbated by… substandard or overcrowded housing. Personal barriers like limited English Proficiency, large families, and the need for two wage earners to provide basic necessities can act as barriers to economic empowerment." [4]

Intergenerational poverty is associated with both the socially and economically induced poverty that continues over multiple generations. Intergenerational poverty robs families of the opportunities needed to ensure future mobility of status for themselves and their children. It transfers past and presents socioeconomic barriers to the next generation and hinders the possibility of acquiring wealth.[5]

"…The aggregate impact of child poverty in the United States leads to reduced skills development and economic productivity, increased crime, and poorer health. "[6] Furthermore, the cognitive effects of poverty on those seeking an education can be profound, leading to social incompetency.[7] These disadvantages are hard to overcome. "[Children] of the disinherited [are] likely to live a heavy life."[8] "Many times, a ceiling is placed on their capacity to dream because of the counsel of despair coming from their elders, whom experience has taught them to expect little and to hope for less."[9] Sadly, approximately fifty percent of American children who are born to parents at the lowest income levels remain there as adults.[10]

As of 2021, Governmental Indices define poverty as an income that does not exceed $26,500 annually for a family of four or $12,880 for an individual.[11] A breakdown of US poverty by race over the age of eighteen shows non-Hispanic whites at 7.3%, African Americans or Blacks at 18.8%, Asians at 7.3%, and Hispanics at 15.7%. The poverty rate among children under 18 is 14.4% which is millions of children. As you can predict, the educational attainment level for families in poverty include "no high school diploma" followed by "only a high school diploma."[12]

Rural poverty has become geographically concentrated in the same way urban poverty is confined by urban neighborhoods.[13] Extreme poverty areas have a trifecta of burden because it touches every aspect of the community to include home, schools, and access to resources.[14]

There is an increasing reliance on taxes in high poverty areas to fund community services and public education. Yet, the tax base is "diminishing," leaving unimaginable tax burden on people who are struggling to maintain their basic needs. [15]

The formula to measure poverty was developed in 1955 and put into use by the federal government in the early sixties. The formula held the cost of food at one-third of a person's pay. The formula, now, factors in inflation but does not consider the rising cost of food, childcare, housing, and healthcare resulting in a very flawed method of measuring poverty. The true matrix could show millions more families who are struggling to survive...let alone thrive.[16]

Poverty at the individual level cannot be separated from the larger social environment. Perpetuating influences that operate in areas with high rates of poverty and multiple barriers cannot be ignored. Also, categorizing a person as "in poverty" or "not in poverty" is one way to describe their economic situation[17] albeit it may be temporary.

Constructing Class and Usurping Power

The problem of poverty is nothing new.[18] Poverty began as an indefinite or unformed concept. "The disproportion of power in a complex society began with the transmutation from the pastoral office to the agrarian economy. This destroyed the simple equalitarian and communism of the hunting and nomadic social organization. It has perpetuated social injustice in every form through all the ages." [19]

The early church understood that the antidote to the poverty concept was piety and sharing. Although there was not a word for poverty[20] in the first four centuries AD, images of the poor conveyed the notion. Once words were attributed to the image of poverty; social hierarchy developed. In Greek texts, two distinct words were used to convey the imagery of the depth of one's poverty. The words used *penēs* and *ptōchos*. "*Ptōchos* traditionally designated the destitute beggar who lived on the fringes of society, the 'street person,' the extreme poor. *Penēs*, on the other hand, was used to indicate the individual whose economic resources were minimal but who functioned within society, 'the working poor'."[21] The Greek word *endeēs* was also used to classify the 'neediness' of an individual.[22]

Penēs could also be used in a derogatory fashion for those members of society who were forced to engage in manual labor for survival. It, moreover, included those who were voluntarily poor. The difference between the two classes of the poor lay in their social ties within the community. P*enētes* maintained their "homes, families and responsibilities."[23] Therefore, *penētes* received a modicum of social standing within the community.

The Hebrew texts used the word *'any* much like *penēs*. The Hebrew term served as an expression that measured how the poor relate to the non-poor members in society. *'Any* were "pressed by debts and dependent (on) the good grace of an employer or creditor."[24] *'Evyon* in the Hebrew is equivalent to the Greek word *ptōchos*. *'Evyon* commonly characterizes a poor person in dire straits. An *'evyon* also needed help immediately if he or she was to survive.

Over time, nuances of the word *ptōchos* were developed to incorporate those who were previously wealthy but "fell into disaster."[25] The meaning of *penēs* expanded to encompass people who "maintain(ed) a stable state of social inferiority and material inadequacy."[26] These nuances solidified the construction of poverty images. The words themselves had nothing to do with one's religious affiliation, and everything to do with a person's social and economic status.[27]

Domination and oppression followed this newfound power structure. "Almost all societies throughout history had both the rich and the poor."[28] The poor are traditionally referenced as an indigent group of people in an undesirable section of society.

In Rome during the fourth century AD, growing gaps between the rich and the poor became more destructive. The transition within the empire over wealth and power created schisms. It proved to be a double-edged sword. This schism affected the political, and social climates within the Roman Empire. On one hand, wealth and power increased. On the other hand, the treatment of the poor changed dramatically as the *ptōchos* and *penēs* were oppressed.

Before Constantine's Empire, people took care of disadvantaged families as a duty outlined by God. Christians viewed the poor as people who simply needed charity and created a community for them. As such, "the church…was gaining a reputation for its charitable work."[29] Because the charitable work of caring for the poor required an abundance of resources, the church soon found it necessary to organize their distribution of goods to the underprivileged.

After Constantine's Empire adopted Christianity, there was a reversal of conditions at the highest level. The relationship became hierarchical. The Roman model of patronage was based on the unconventional relationship the patronus (guardian, protector) and his client (the poor). Leaders took on the responsibility to administering the funds and overseeing the distribution of properties to those in need. For the first time the "role of benefactor and leader" was combined.[30] Absolute authority over the poor and complete access to funding created an excuse to dominate the lower class.

Ironically, we often hear a call for the separation of church (small c as this relates to the institution and not the Body of Christ) and State as a measure of prohibiting religion from overtaking the State. However, in this instance, the State sullied the church. The church has never fully recovered.

From the fourth century AD forward, the powerful – and not necessarily Christians – claimed authority over the disadvantaged people of society. Poverty became a way of defining people's lives instead of a circumstance or economic predicament.[31] Almsgiving became a thing of the past. The state of poverty came to be viewed as a punishment for sin, and it was felt that sinners should not receive charity. This new ideology, however flawed, made individuals at fault for poverty. If you make poverty or oppression the fault of the oppressed, you can 1) rationalize the need for domination 2) feel morally justified in their suffering i.e. if they did what we did, their situation would not be this way.

Nations throughout history have used and continue to use class domination in one form or another to gain power and wealth. The truth is someone's need for wealth and power oppresses those less wealthy and powerful – from the Pharaoh and the Israelites to the Roman Empire to King Louis and Versailles to America and racial segregation. This is a formula. It has become the narrative of those in power to devalue and dominate others to maintain social power.

As Reinhold Niebuhr observes, [Napoleon] "could bathe Europe in the blood for the sake of gratifying his overweening lust for power, as long as he could pose as the tool of French patriotism and as the instrument of revolutionary fervor. ... [Napoleon] "would have not been permitted to indulge this vanity however had it not seemed compatible with the prejudices of his people and the economic necessities of a growing empire."[32] Hate is a mechanism of control. Hatred becomes quite respectable even though it has to masquerade often under the guise of patriotism.[33] Patriotism transmutes individual unselfishness into national egoism.[34]

In America, we are radically divided by race, gender, and economics, and we seem to be all too comfortable with the outcomes. Furthermore, race, class, and gender identity are things one cannot control at birth.

Dr. Gregory Mantsios says, "When you look at society and try to determine what it is that keeps most people down – what holds them back from realizing their potential as healthy, creative, productive individuals – you find institutional forces that are largely beyond individual control. Class domination is one of these forces." [35] Moreover, opportunities are lessened by these constructs.

Many people choose to deny that class standing is the root of wealth, prosperity, power, and occupational roles. As Mantsios argues, however,

> from the cradle to the grave, class standing has a significant and indefinite impact on our chances for survival. The lower one's class standing, the more difficult it is to secure appropriate housing, the more time is spent on the routine tasks of everyday life, the greater is the percentage of income that goes to pay for food, rent/housing and other basic necessities, and the greater is the likelihood of crime victimization.[36]

Dr. Mantsios argues further, in the essay *Class in America,* "the idea that everyone has an equal chance to succeed" is a great fabrication. "It is the American culture to ignore the idea of social class because this belief flies in the face of the 'American dream' or equal opportunity for all."[37] In an HBO Special, Comedian George Carlin joked that "it is called the American Dream because you have to be asleep to believe it."[38]

The legitimacy of the belief that success in America only requires "sacrifice, hard work, and perseverance leads one to ask several important questions. Are there significant class differences among Americans? If these differences exist, are they getting bigger or smaller, and do these differences have a significant impact on the way we live? Finally, does everyone in the United States really have an equal opportunity to succeed?"[39]

The fact is, working hard is no guarantee of upward mobility. "The greatness of the United States [is] that it provides [a] degree of equality 'without destroying the necessary subordination."[40] The starting place and systemic challenges separate the upward mobility of the disadvantaged.

"The privileged class... [invents] romantic and moral interpretations of the real facts, preferring to obscure rather than reveal the true character of their collective behavior." [41] I have noticed the privileged feeling justified in telling stories of how hard their grandparents and parents worked as if disadvantaged people did not come from a long line of hard workers.

On one hand, "the most common form of hypocrisy among the privileged classes is to assume that their privileges are the just payments with which society rewards especially useful or meritorious functions. ...it is always possible for social privilege to justify itself, at least in its own eyes... ... [for] classes who possess hereditary advantages, it must be proved or assumed that the underprivileged classes would not have the capacity of rendering the same service [outcome] if given the opportunity."[42]

"On the other hand, it has always been the habit of the privileged groups to deny the [repressed] classes every opportunity for the cultivation of innate capacities and then accusing them of lacking what they have been denied the right to acquire." [43]

This also helps people with biases validate their reasoning for passing judgment.

In 2020, Wells Fargo CEO Charles Scharf publicly expressed "trouble reaching diversity goals because there is not enough qualified minority talent."[44] To that Lauren Holland replied, "The talent is there. It's a matter of the firm assessing it and connecting with it."[45]

I vividly remember one year I was selected to participate in a national competition. I wrote a detailed essay outlining my story and why I chose Community Ministry. I was selected as the winner of an Award from Outstanding Pastoral Leadership. I was flown to Texas to accept the award. It was one of the most exciting moments of my life. Afterward, I was approached by a member of the voting committee in the hotel lobby. She was so proud of me but a professor standing nearby blurted out, "she did not come here this smart, we made her that way." He followed the statement with a grand chuckle. I was shocked. Where did that come from? Thankfully, she ignored him and his remark. She encouraged me to keep going. I sat silently in my hotel room internalizing his comments for the rest of the evening.

I wish I knew then what I know now. I have, since, learned of the farce in the ideology of being less than anyone as it pertains to class, education, employment, and the like. It creates an air of subservience that was manufactured long ago. To paraphrase Dr. Martin Luther King, Jr., the idea of superiority and inferiority of anyone is a myth and given equal opportunities, everyone could demonstrate equal achievement. The danger of perpetuating the inferiority myth is living a lie as truth nullifies value on both sides. Are you superior because you make everyone else inferior? Or are you dominant based on your own merit?

My view is that the wealthy are interconnected and dependent on the working-class. Without the workers, the rich would have to perform the laborious tasks themselves. Perhaps they would not be as wealthy or acquire wealth as quickly.

Working-class people struggle in their own lives because they are not being paid what they are worth and become indebted as a result. The dominant culture continues to perpetuate the idea of superiority by further creating the idea of ownership. American theologian and ethicist, Reinhold Niebuhr states, "Few people can look at a problem related to social policy and not think of their own interests. Humankind will never forego the problems of equity especially since it means preservation and personal fulfillment. Classes may be formed based on common functions in society, but they do not become sharply distinguished until function is translated into privilege."[46] This mindset of superiority is ingrained in the psyche of the dominant culture even in the absence of wealth and power.

Underprivileged families are left to find ways to act on behalf of themselves without the adequate amount of power or ability. "There is one overmastering problem that the socially and politically disinherited always face: Under what terms is survival possible when you are forced to live under hostility?"[47] That would prove to be an especially important question.

Humanity "has not yet learned how to live together

without compounding their vices and covering each other 'with mud and with blood.'"[48]   One group would almost always yield to another. Those in lower socioeconomic groups are forced to yield to the power of the majority. To paraphrase theologian Reinhold Niebuhr, humanity's aptitude for fairness makes justice possible however, their natural predisposition to injustice makes democracy necessary. Democracy meaning the opposite of fascism.

In short, the spirit of man is innately created with a sense of justice. We live in a world of right and wrong. However, humanity is always at war with the flesh. The natural desire of the flesh is self-gratification. Therefore, there is always a willingness to disenfranchise others for personal fulfillment. "Watch and pray so that you will not fall into temptation. The spirit is willing, but the flesh is weak." Matthew 26:41 (NIV) This makes democracy necessary.

Chapter 3

The Masterplan

vs.

the Master's Plan

The earth is the Lord's, and everything in it, the world,
and all who live in it; for he founded it on the seas
and established it on the waters. Who may ascend the
mountain of the Lord? Who may stand in his holy place?

Psalm 24:1-3 NIV

I had the privilege of working within local government in Allendale, South Carolina. I worked alongside the Mayor, Town Administrator, Chief of Police, and Municipal Council members. For reference, Allendale, South Carolina was burned to the ground during the Civil War and rebuilt in 1873. Since that time, the town's economic system rested on agricultural crops. A big boom occurred in Allendale in the 1940's and 50's, when the main highway, U.S. 301, was developed. Allendale was conveniently located between New York and Florida and travelers found Allendale to be a perfect stopping point.

The town was changed forever in 1960 when I-95 was planned and constructed 35 miles to the East. As travelers began using the newly constructed Interstate to commute south, Allendale's tourism industry collapsed. Poverty levels as well as unemployment rose. By the 1970's, the Allendale, South Carolina region became known as one of the poorest and least educated corridors in the state.[49]

Because of my position, disgruntled residents of Allendale would scream at me anywhere they saw me – in the grocery store, at a stop sign, at a local eatery, even while taking out the trash. They were upset about their utility bill and property taxes. I do not think it mattered to them that I had zero control over any of it.

The residents of Allendale had been suffering for a long time with decades of high unemployment rates and crippling poverty.

My duties in the municipal offices included multiple functions as I worked jointly with the Allendale County Tax Department collecting outstanding tax debts. One of my first assignments included interviewing a public official for a newsletter. The white official – quite comfortably – explained the history of Allendale. I will never forget his statement that desegregating schools was the worst thing to ever happen to Allendale. He continued, "It causes white flight which in turn is why Allendale was poor." I sat quietly not sure what to say after his statement. This incident set the tone for life in the South.

One morning, I was asked to create the marketing presentation for the town's Masterplan. The town officials were spearheading a beautification project. The Masterplan outlined neighborhood expansions. At the time, I did not think to ask, "what would happen to the existing businesses and structures?" I had never heard of a Masterplan prior to working on the presentation. Until this point, my work in the community had been limited to the role of a direct service provider for maternal child health.

The town's public officials created a plan to attract young people to this once bustling town. The officials dreamed of Allendale becoming a college town. Local businesses such as new eateries, a financial institution, coffee shops, a biking trail and new shrubbery on the roadways were incorporated into the community plan.

I learned, much later, how the "Masterplan" works. Here is a brief synopsis of how a Masterplan is created. The Planning Board creates a Masterplan which designs the desired appearance of the city to include what type of homes can be built, how many retail shops are allowed and where, how much open space is desired or needed, etc. The Masterplan becomes a guiding document to create land use laws or ordinances.

The plan prepares for population growth, community development, open spaces, etc. Land use planning influences the way local government determines what is allowed in a particular area based on the *Land Use Planning Guide*. The

Masterplan for Allendale included removing blighted housing, adding commercial assets and streetscaping for an uncertain future. The Mayor of Allendale sought to do his due diligence by asking for community participation. However, the focus of the masterplan, in my opinion, was on design and neglected the well-being of the existing community.

Other states like New Jersey, refer to district planning as the Municipal Land Use Law (MLUL). "The MLUL is the legislation that enables municipal land use and development planning, zoning, and historic preservation zoning."[50] The MLUL also describes and codifies the roles and responsibilities of the municipal governing body, Planning and Zoning Boards in land use administration. "Municipalities identify, evaluate, designate, and regulate individual sites and districts under the Municipal Land Use Law (MLUL)."[51]

Planning and zoning are regulated on a local level. The Municipal Land Use Law or other planning guides enable townships to establish their own development rules through the adoption of a Zoning Ordinance and a Zoning Map.[52]

The ordinances and map are companion documents that determine what can be built or exist within a community. The map shows the limits of each of the zones that have been established by action of the local governing body. The zoning ordinance provides the specifics of what may exist in each zone.[53] Ordinances are passed and put the Masterplan into effect.

Use variances are needed to allow use of a property not permitted in a particular zone. A use variance requires the applicant to prove hardship to the property due to the stringent ordinance as well as the benefit to the community. Property owners may have to get legal representation, property experts, and make tens of thousands of dollars' worth of changes without a guarantee of approval. A conditional use permit does not require the proof of hardship and authorizes property use conditionally. However, municipalities have the power to refuse to allow conditional use variances.

In short, the municipality can build or block business, homes, eateries, shopping centers, support facilities, etc. in accordance with their individual Masterplan.

The Masterplan

As a young writer, my first article, published by Associated Baptist Press, tackled the issue of Master-planning in a community that was on the verge of displacing the displaced. The homeless shelter was an eye sore that needed to relinquish its position for luxury condos. The "Master-planned" development sold a hot item in an otherwise slow real estate market in metro-Atlanta. Developers offer a "city inside a city" experience without the cookie-cutter detached houses of suburbia. The developers of the Master Plan sold dreams of increased social activity in dilapidated neighborhoods to young professionals.

"Yay! Revenue!" But what is the real cost? There is a downside of living in a world where if it does not make money, it does not make sense. It implies that if one does not make dollars, one life is only worth a few cents. Is this really the Master's plan? Isn't it that same selfishness that contributed to the present plight of urban neighborhoods? How about decisions to insert highways and railways through urban neighborhoods?"[54] Those choices continue to contribute to the poverty within less fortunate neighborhoods.

Let us not forget that once upon a time, the Masterplan sold the populace "flight" as a means of segregation, as well as revitalization for gentrification. Richard Rothstein, author of *The Color of Law*, describes a tactic that was used to prevent the so-called Negro invasion of Wayne, New Jersey by residents of Paterson, New Jersey. Defense against the "Negro Invasion" barred residents of Paterson from moving into wealthier areas of Wayne, New Jersey. The "Negro invasion"[55] marketed racial fear in housing and education and sold the notion of reduced property value to gain property at a discounted rate from white property owners.[56]

The developers then sold white families on new suburban developments while increasing the cost of their previous homes to sell to African American families, i.e. increasing property value.[57] Isn't it ironic that green is the only color that matters in the buying and selling of fear? Green is also the overarching hue in revitalization and displacement.

Gentrification has become a buzz word when discussing vulnerable community redevelopment. Gentrification is redevelopment that caters to the taste of middle America, thereby displacing renters and homeowners who can no longer afford to live in the neighborhood. Redevelopment efforts have caused greater misfortune for families too poor to remain in their neighborhood. You can readily begin to realize the inequity in the Masterplan.

Whether rural, urban, or suburban, a Masterplan – coupled with inequity and inadequate governmental representation – dictates what and/or who your neighborhood would resemble. Would the community have single-family homes, two family homes, multi-units housing structures, or apartment buildings?

The reverse, hence, is creating an equitable Masterplan in high poverty areas. An equitable Masterplan in high-poverty neighborhoods should be 'people-based' and 'place-based.'[58] "Having people-based initiatives helps to break the cycle of poverty."[59] Also, rebuilding neighborhoods should consist of expanding educational and economic opportunities for residents. Because you cannot try to fix people without fixing the overarching problems that create poverty, the Masterplan should entail advocating for legislation that stabilizes the most vulnerable communities.

Often the community leaders who are making decisions in inequitable communities are not directly affected by the community changes. The residents live under the weight of the decisions. This is a model that is mimicked from the highest level of government down to the lowest.

The Master's Plan

Jeremiah 29:11 (NIV) tells us that the Master "plans to prosper you and not to harm you, plans to give you hope and a future." The Master's plan is one of redemption by the sacrificing of God's one and only son. The Master's plan is never one of subjugation. The municipality's plan can be destructive and exclusionary, but God's plan is restorative and inclusionary.

Municipal decision makers can decide to build senior housing a few feet away from an active transit overpass resulting in violent shaking of apartments. Or erect luxury condos in a flood zone, in an industrial area, or near the city dump. Or permit twice the state recommended number of liquor stores and unhealthy eateries to exist in a city. These decisions mimic the post-civil war era practice of building up ghettos around undesirable structures. "It is not uncommon to see rebuilt public housing surrounded by failing schools or even other troubled housing, rife with lead hazards and asthma triggers."[60] The decision makers and developers, however, are gaining financially.

Many urban centers experience these phenomena. Not only are the luxury properties made cheaply, but maintenance is also impossible due to the external factors like flooding and transit shaking. On top of this, the spirits stores and eateries can operate to the wee hours of the morning attracting people from neighboring areas because this is not allowed in their area. This breeds crime and leads to flight for those who can afford to leave.

All of these external forces contribute to continued poverty in the community. However, the people who live in these communities are led to believe that they are the cause of the poverty in the community. The most impressive deception is making the community believe that the aforementioned modifications are upgrades. Officials try to convince families that they are getting more than they had previously and more than they deserve. "There are few things more devastating than to have it burned into you that you do not count and that no provisions are made for literal protection of your person. Under such circumstance there is but a step between being despised and despising oneself." [61] Perhaps this is the Masterplan.

But there is nothing new under the sun. The first chapters of the book of Exodus tell the story of a new king coming into power over Egypt. The new king looks at a group of people and creates a narrative about them. The king may have thought, "The Israelites are now 51% of the population and we are 49%. They may continue to multiply and overtake us. We have to do something." This is one example of a lie the king had to sell himself and others in order to feel imaginarily attacked enough to justify oppression.

A war was now waged in the minds of the actual dominant culture unbeknownst to the other groups. The Israelites were simply living their lives apart from the king's newfound perception. The leadership resented a people group through no fault of their own. The king, in turn, took the Israelites' possessions, enslaved them, and devised a plan to kill off the males. By the way, today, different minority groups comprise under 40% of America's population and non-minorities account for over 60% of the population as of 2018. [62] However, the 51-49 percentage is an untruth I hear frequently among the dominant culture in America.

When we get to Exodus chapter 5, the once strong prosperous people are now labeled as lazy and inferior. The monarchy managed to erase and rewrite the history of the people. They replaced a rich heritage with a false narrative and stigmatized a people group in the process. The Israelites were working harder than before with less help and materials when they were called lazy. This is a form of ownership. Ownership allows people in power to enslave, kill and change the narrative of a people group while omitting their history. The text of Exodus depicts hard-working people with little opportunity for upward mobility. The misconception promulgated by the entities in power kept the people self-repressed. [63] Furthermore, the Egyptian people benefit from the king's oppression of the Israelites whether they wanted to admit it or not. There is an adage based on Jeremiah 5:21 KJV, which states, there is none so blind as those who won't see.

Social exclusionism is the "ism" that follows to further justify exclusion based on the new narrative. The impact of *that* master's plan, per the new sociopolitical system, does not demonstrate the hopes of God, who is the true Master.

Moses embodied leaders who strove to carry out God's ultimate plan. Moses chose God and leadership within the community. Moses' divine assignment confronted Pharaoh's destructive plan and uplifted the plan of God which is salvation and freedom.

This is where my divinely appointed calling hit its highest point. I realized that like Moses, I have a Mosaic calling to be a voice for the disadvantaged and marginalized. Moses was the first community advocate according to the dynamics of Exodus 5. Moses, in Exodus 5 could be understood as a freeing agent for a particular group of people[64] who felt a "sense of helplessness because of an uninformed legislative system." [65]

Moses was seeking a sociopolitical transformation. I am called to facilitate complex collaborative conversations between the community and the power source. I am working as someone who has lived among both groups of people. I realize the hurdles involved in first breaking through stereotypes[66] as well as recognizing that the second hurdle is being patient and persistent when leadership make promises to pacify the challengers without eradicating the oppression.

As we saw in 2020, when some companies like Quaker Oats decided to rebrand passé images like Aunt Jemima opposed to committing to making real systemic change regarding race. Meanwhile, subjugated people are living between two powerful polarities: Spiritual Oppression and Spiritual Depression. Spiritual Oppression is caused by systemic subjugation and the brutal, unjust manner people in power treat those who are less fortunate or different. It can be viewed as cultural chauvinism. Cultural chauvinism is the belief that one's culture is superior, and acts are performed to exert supremacy. "The psychological price of loyalty to one's own group can be hostility toward another, especially when there is a long history of enmity between the groups." [67] Spiritual oppression by one group or agency over another creates spirited depression in the subjected group or community.

Spiritual oppression includes laws and legislation that justify discriminatory practices, inequity in housing, over-policing poorer neighborhoods, voter suppression, and the like. As Martin Luther King and others teach "to deprive a man of freedom is to relegate him to the status of a thing, rather than elevate him to the status of a person."[68]

Spiritual depression is the result of negative spiritual forces that create an air of hopelessness. It evokes a strong feeling of discouragement, despair, or apathy that can last a lifetime. Spiritual depression is the direct result of decades of being slandered and held down until one believes they are inferior. You will be surprised how oppression is passed down generationally. Minds held captive are hard to change.

Dr. Martin Luther King Jr. says,

"Many unconsciously wondered whether they actually deserve better… Their minds and souls {are} conditioned to the system of segregation that they submissively {adjust} themselves to things as they {are}. …It not only hurts people physically, but also hurts people mentally. It inflects the segregated with a false sense of inferiority, while confirming the segregator in a false estimate of his superiority. It is a system which forever stares the {other} in the face, saying: 'You are less than…' 'You are not equal to…'"[69]

Racism and the Civil War

I remember a candid conversation I had with a friend of mine about Barack Obama and living while black. My friend is white by the way. I repeated what a woman in South

Carolina told me about the reason for racism and why black people are hated and treated poorly. The South Carolinian woman explained to me that racism stemmed from the Civil War. She stated that the slaves, i.e., Black people, destroyed white southerners' way of life. She continued that slavery was economics and Black people made it personal. I was expecting my friend to dissent against the notion. Instead she said, "there is some truth to that." My stomach sank. This is an example of legitimizing hate of a racial group based on an untruth as a way of blaming the victim.

Her next statement almost made my head do a 180-degree spin and cause my chin to rest on the nape of my neck. "But Angela," she continued, "**you do not have to worry about that because** you have earned the right to speak. You have made something of yourself. Other minorities who are not as productive, really cannot speak. Lower class black people like the people in Decatur, Georgia feel entitled to a right that they do not have because their dependency on the 'system'." She continued to tell me how uncouth other black people were but not me.

There is nothing more entitling than feeling like you can bestow and remove a human being's "right" to speak as well as any inalienable rights. "Enjoying the moral pleasure of giving what does not belong to them and the practical advantage of withholding enough to preserve their eminence {is a form of} superiority."[70]

One can indelibly assume the reign of ownership hereby "giving and withholding" inalienable rights. In essence, a black person who is deemed 'unproductive,' by an impalpable matrix, can have his or her voice nullified making their human rights revokable.

I realized in that moment that indoctrinated prejudices especially occurring early in life are hard to eradicate. Even when benign or non-threatening racists disavow racism, they still may act out covert biases.

A benign racist is a seemingly progressive thinker on the outside but who is saturated with antiquated conservative ideologies on the inside. People remember more readily instances that support biases while tending to discount the instances that challenge the narrative. [71] Therefore, if a negative stereotype is observed, it tends to reflect the entire people group. However, if someone of the same people group wins a high honor, it is just an individual act achieved by one stellar standout. This is another form of ownership, i.e., I create your value as a person.

Malignant or dangerous and deadly racists, on the other hand, justify the killing of other races and people as a means of self-preservation. Remember, malignant racists who worshipped the Lord, left the church to become a part of the lynching and brutalize God's creation, then returned to church. This phenomenon was so prevalent that American theologian Reinhold Niebuhr notably stated, "If there were a lynching, I would bet ten to one a church member was in it."[72] Church leaders found ways – however ill-founded – to justify lynchings.

Malignant racists often classify themselves as Christian. However, is it ever acceptable to raise blood-stained hands to the Lord? Racism is not the way of Christ. Racism, and all of its mutations, is a man-made cancer.

I often regretted not continuing the conversation with my friend. I was too offended at the time to revisit or appreciate the conversation. My friend was open enough to be honest about her feelings with me. However, I was too hurt and saddened to ever have another conversation until this day. But, in the spirit of Maya Angelou, in racism whether malignant or benign, count it all joy when people tell you who they are outright.

In 2019, I had another impromptu conversation with an associate after a work function. I made a statement that if we all practiced treating human beings like human beings then racism or hate would not exist. To which she immediately replied, **"But Angela, that is the hardest part."** If I never hear "But Angela" followed by a statement that was gut-wrenchingly painful again, it will still be two times too many. As painful as her statement was to hear, it made perfect sense based on the mistreatment of and justification of mistreatment by those who practice racism.

As the story from Genesis tells us, God gave humanity dominion over animals and instructions to tend to the Earth. People were never intended to have dominion over people. It was never intended for man to relegate humanity into forced dominion. Man chose that structure, not God. This is not a God ordained structure.

Then God said, "Let us make mankind in our image, in our likeness, so that they may rule over the fish in the sea and the birds in the sky, over the livestock and all the wild animals, and over all the creatures that move along the ground." So God created mankind in his own image, in the image of God he created them; male and female he created them. God blessed them and said to them, "Be fruitful and increase in number; fill the earth and subdue it. Rule over the fish in the sea and the birds in the sky and over every living creature that moves on the ground." Then God said, "I give you every seed-bearing plant on the face of the whole earth and every tree that has fruit with seed in it. They will be yours for food. And to all the beasts of the earth and all the birds in the sky and all the creatures that move along the ground—everything that has the breath of life in it—I give every green plant for food." And it was so. Genesis 1:26-30 NIV

In the book *Soul Making*, Alan Jones outlines two ways of understanding Christian conversions. The first is integration and the second is turned upside down. Integrators allow the Spirit of God to permeate their soul. This integration causes the individual to do the hard work to overcome intransigent attitudes. Turned upside down conversion are people who simply place Christ on top of their biases with no measure of integration. Upside down conversion leads to rigidity and a destructive kind of exclusivity.[73]

In the case of the American Civil War, forced labor, torture, rape, lynching and systemic dehumanization are personal to the person on the receiving end. My understanding of the

Civil War and Abraham Lincoln's emancipation of the slaves is that it had little to do with humanity toward the slaves. President Lincoln strove to bring the South into subjection. As a result, freeing the slaves depleted the southern economy weakening the southern states. As Dr. Martin Luther King Jr. said, "Emancipation was a Proclamation but not a fact. The pen of the Great Emancipator had moved the Negro into the sunlight of physical freedom, but actual conditions had left him behind in the shadow of political, psychological, social, economic, and intellectual bondage."[74]

Lincoln made his view plain, "I am not, nor ever have been in favor of bringing about in anyway the social and political equality of the white and black races...there must be the position of superior and inferior, and I as much as any other man am in favor of having the superior position assigned to the white race."[75] As per historian Sarah Pruitt, Lincoln also "opposed blacks having the right to vote, to serve on juries, to hold office and to intermarry with whites."[76] Lincoln was assassinated before the world could definitively interpret Lincoln's sympathies toward Black people as a true change of heart. Furthermore, the South never recovered economically and remains the poorest region in the United States.

Additionally, I cringe when people talk about cutting taxes as a means of "ensuring dollars" do not go to help minorities or those in need. This mentality comes from slavery and the feeling of ownership through status. People who utilize safety net programs are often employed and are paying taxes as well.

Paying taxes does not give you authority over people's lives, it saves you from the IRS and prison.

Also, if there were no safety net programs, you will probably be paying the same amount of taxes. Surprise! Ta-da! If more people shared opportunities then no one would have to figmentally lord over others because the opposite of poverty is justice as stated by Bryan Stevenson in his TED Talk titled, *We need to talk about an Injustice.*[77]

Another fact about ownership is 'you cannot price yourself out of the isms of the world' as Gabrielle Union so eloquently put it in her interview *Pricing out of Racism.*[78] "The treatment of black people in America, and the ways in which we are perceived, vilified and punished for merely wanting to be valued as human beings." [79] Social exclusionism is often coupled with racism, sexism, or classism. It serves as a measure of putting one in their place. Therefore, the ideology behind ownership and social exclusion is not about poverty, it is about privilege. The laws are created to mirror these sentiments.

Present Day Injustices

Historically, laws have reinforced the 'isms' in America realizing "much of the criminal justice system was built, honed and firmly established during the Jim Crow era."[80] These laws were state and local regulations that legalized racial segregation. The Jim Crow laws existed for about 100 years— from the post-Civil War era until 1968— to "marginalize African Americans by denying them the right to vote, hold jobs, get an education or other opportunities. Those who attempted to defy Jim Crow laws often faced arrest, fines, jail sentences, violence, and death." [81]

There are unignorable problems within the circuitry of the law that is connected to race. Here are a few examples highlighted by Radley Balko in the article, *There's Overwhelming Evidence that the Criminal Justice System is Racist*:

- 'Black people are almost twice as likely to be pulled over as whites, black people are more likely to be searched following a stop,' and about four times as likely to be searched despite the fact they are less likely to be found with contraband."

- "The Black arrest rate is at least twice as high as the white arrest rate for disorderly conduct, drug possession, simple assault, theft, vagrancy, and vandalism."

- Black people are consistently arrested, charged, and convicted of drug crimes including possession, distribution, and conspiracy at far higher rates than white people. This, despite research showing that both races use and sell drugs at about the same rate.

- "Dynamic entry" and paramilitary police tactics are disproportionately used against Black and Latino people. Most of these raids were on people suspected of low-level drug crimes. However, Police were more successful in recovering the targeted drugs from white suspects.

- "Disparities in policing and punishment within the black population along the color continuum exceed disparities between blacks and whites as a whole. That is, the darker the skin of a black person, the greater the disparity in arrests, charges, conviction rates and sentencing.

- Race plays a role at nearly every step in the process, from arrest to detention to setting bail to sentencing.

- White, non-Hispanics, make up about 60 percent of the U.S. population, they comprise 83% of state trial court judges and 80 percent of state appellate court judges. 95% of elected prosecutors are white, and nearly 80 percent are white men.[82]

The list could go on ad infinitum to include suspension of minority students more often resulting in children being forced into the prison pipeline, disparity in the diversity of parole officers leading to higher reincarceration rates, and reporting of the minority city's gang while white supremacist gangs appear to be significantly under-included.[83]

My point in stating all of the above is to shine a light on the legal after-effects. I have known people who were formerly incarcerated for a drug offense to be restricted from receiving federal funding for student loans. These same individuals are barred from public or affordable housing in a better neighborhood because of the conviction. Certain convictions mandated an automatic driver's license suspension even if the person never had a driver's license. Incredibly, if you lack one, the Department of Motor Vehicles will create a driver's license number for you and suspend it. From the suspension, a restoration fee as well as other fees are charged and attached to a license they never had. New Jersey is one of twelve states that imposes a mandatory license suspension for some drug offenses. Finally, they were ineligible to vote while on parole or probation. This law has been changed in some states, but the damage is done. These laws stifle rehabilitation and full participation in society.

A formerly incarcerated person can be barred from higher education, housing, childcare, medical care, etc., prohibiting rehabilitation. This disproportionately affects people of color and people in poverty.

I encountered the ways of the law at 15 years old. I was on a bus with my friends and acquaintances on my way home. Suddenly, an altercation broke out. I was familiar with both parties in the altercation, but I was unaware of any ill-feelings. During the commotion, I remained seated. Things settled down after a while and I was able to make it home without incident. A few weeks later, I received a notice in the mail regarding the bus altercation. I was stunned. I was guilty by association, but I was innocent. My mom took me to the hearing, and we went into a little room to speak with the public defender. I told him everything. I stated that I was innocent. I did not do anything, and I remained in my seat. This pale skinned gray-haired man looked at me and told me that I had to say I was guilty. He went on to tell my mom how we could not fight it and if we did, I could go to jail – that was my public defense. My public defender advised me to commit perjury, as

I now know, by creating a story of events. He rehearsed with me what I had to tell the judge. I was convinced to plead guilty and lied about my guilt as per the public defender. I received six months' probation and a court date for a review hearing for remaining seated with my hands in my lap during an altercation.

The first meeting with my probation officer Mr. 'Thomas,' was strange. I told him I was innocent but was told to plead guilty by the Public Defender. He just listened. At the second meeting, he said I never had to see him again because he knew "I did not belong there." Six months later, the judge agreed and sealed my record. The guilty plea had the propensity to destroy my life. To this day, I have no idea what charge I pled guilty to. People will take advantage of the things you do not know. As an aside, there were more younger people in the room pleading guilty with me who were not so lucky. Those who did poorly in school were kept on probation. So, the first time they made a mistake years later; it resulted in immediate jail time.

Now, race is not the only factor to worry about in the criminal justice system. To be fair, as Balko recognizes:

"White people are wrongly accused, arrested and convicted. White people are treated unfairly, beaten, and unjustifiably shot and killed by police officers. White people too are harmed by policies such as mandatory minimums, asset forfeiture, and abuse of police, prosecutorial and judicial power."[84]

Money and power also play a huge role in what kind of

justice is served. Creators of the law, government, high-ranking officials, and their friends are not held accountable the way an ordinary citizen would be. There is an unspoken rule. We make the laws, but we do not follow the laws. Perhaps this is why people like Jeffrey Epstein are able to sexually abuse and traffic children for decades after numerous complaints to the authorities– as per the Netflix documentary *Jeffrey Epstein: Filthy Rich* – and remain free. Jeffrey had the privilege of having friends who made but circumvented the law.

One of my favorite movies of all times is "Devil's Advocate." Al Pacino, who plays the Devil, explains the advantages of embedding himself in the law. "You build egos the size of Cathedrals; fiber-optically connect the world to every ego impulse; grease even the dullest dreams … until every human becomes an aspiring Emperor that becomes his own God. And you go from there."[85] The dialogue continues, "Why the law?" "Cause the law my boy puts us into everything. It's the ultimate backstage pass. It's the new priesthood, baby." [86]

Subjugated communities do not have the luxury of not understanding the law. We continually witness laws and legislation used against marginalized people. Moreover, there "will always run the peril of introducing new forms of injustice in place of those abolished." [87]

A plan was created for our life that was generated decades before you were born. That is the Masterplan but is it the *Master's plan?* Someone attempted to plan the outcome before our parents planned us. However, no person's or group's plan tops the real Master's plan. King's mother said, "you must never feel like you are less than anyone else." "You must always feel like you are somebody." Even when the systems around you do not match.

I remember a clip from entertainer Meek Mill challenging the people living in derelict environments to "move their mind." Meek Mill is a prominent entertainer from Philadelphia, Pennsylvania. He experienced the prison system at an early age and managed to become a multi-millionaire before the age of 30. However, being a successful artist was not enough to prevent injustices to him by the legal system. Today, Meek Mill is dedicated to prison reform and making positive changes in the community.

My interpretation of the phrase "move your mind" is that possibilities are more abundant if your mind is free. If you do not "think freely" you **may** begin to kill, steal, and destroy as a way of gaining materials or to create a false sense of escapism from entrapment by oppressing other people. Destruction by forcibly taking control of other's possessions seems to be the most common form of destruction and leads to all sorts of dominating and threatening behaviors.[88]

I am pointing out destructive behaviors because I encountered two seven-year-olds while speaking to children in a church in South Carolina. Before I could say anything, the first seven-year-old wanted to know how much money I made. "Are you rich?" "No," I replied. "Well, I need to know how to get this money." How old are you?" I asked. "Seven," he answered very matter of fact. "In this space, I need you to be seven and not think about 'getting this money,' I answered. I could not imagine the weight on the shoulders of this seven-year-old. He felt like it was his responsibility to take care of his sisters and family. At seven-years-old, he was already looking for a way out of what he was experiencing in the neighborhood.

The next session, with, yet another seven-year-old, was much more intense. This tiny little fella was so brazen. He told me flat out, "I need a gun." My mouth flew open. I asked, "Why do you think you need a gun?" He said "because I do. Whether I go to the army or I am in the streets, I need a gun." My eyes welled up. I spent the next hour trying to uproot a deeply rooted belief that guns were the way out.

We have seven-year-olds trying to figure out life. My parents had to figure it out with a fourth and sixth grade education, respectively. How are seven-year-olds going to navigate life with a second-grade education? They are probably navigating based on what they see – i.e. guns and getting money by whatever way is available.

As Meek said, "renew your mind" despite the odds because, as I have observed, there are children watching you. It is not an easy process, but it can be done. Please hear me, this is in addition to advocating for what you believe in. One cannot believe that the circumstances of our society are too complex and difficult to be changed. The truth is your life may have started 'here' but it does not have to end 'here'.

I had a lot to overcome. I had to realize that subjugation was not God's plan for me, but I faced some hard lessons in the process.

Chapter 4

Validation

Am I now trying to win the approval of human beings,
or of God? Or am I trying to please people? If I were still
trying to please people, I would not be a servant of Christ.

Galatians 1:10 NIV

❧

After two years of seeing the residents of the city struggling with just about every basic necessity, I wanted to make a deeper impact on the community in Allendale, South Carolina. I had a draft manuscript of a children's book and an idea to start a nonprofit publishing company which gave back to the community. My call was ever-present, and all roads led me to seminary. This became my second bout with homelessness. I was accepted into seminary and I moved to Georgia without a plan. Yes, I repeated a cycle. I knew God put me there and I trusted the Lord's leading. I remember attending orientation during the second week of August 2009 and I had no idea where I would sleep that night.

Ade is a Christian woman I was introduced to through a mutual friend. Our friend connected us as we were both new to the area. Ade had an apartment that contained an air mattress. That night, two complete strangers – Ade and her friend – shared their queen size air mattress with me as we each pursued our dreams.

On campus, I felt lost and socially isolated. I felt like a total outcast. I wore ripped, tight jeans and big earrings. I remember someone telling me that these characteristics helped him remember who I was. "You are the girl with the big, funky earrings and ripped, tight jeans." I knew he did not mean any harm by his comment, but my heart sank. I felt as if my urbanization made me stand out and, in that moment, I had never felt more left behind.

I was not your quintessential seminary student, as I am still not your conventional minister. I did not believe I belonged in seminary. I prayed often for God to choose a friend of mine versus me. I had a list of reasons why she would be a much better fit than me. I knew I was called to community but an MPA or MPH would do me fine. But seminary? Jesus…?

In seminary, I was faced with abstractions that were supposed to make sense of my life's experiences. It was incredibly challenging. My beliefs were being tested daily. Hermeneutics and other theological verbiage filled the classroom. I scurried to my next class to find Biblical Greek. Quite frankly, everything was a foreign language. As some professors became comfortable with the students, other conversations occurred.

One afternoon a professor, walked into class and said, "Only my African-American students answer. I am talking to my African American students. I have been watching a fascinating show called *The Wire*...Is it true?" He stared excitedly at the class, looking around the room waiting for an answer.

For those of you that do not know, *The Wire* was a show about drug dealing and violence in Baltimore, Maryland. I have never watched *The Wire* but knew the underlying assumption. We are African Americans therefore we know about drugs and violence in dilapidated neighborhoods. Although I was from an impoverished neighborhood, I never experienced the drug culture. Needless to say, no one answered the professor. Since "criminality and delinquency are not racial," [89] I am sure others in the room may have had the answer this professor sought.

Let me say, my writing about different educators and others is not to criticize anyone. I love my educational experiences and personal ties. I am, merely, highlighting life-altering events that show how racial biases are ingrained in even the lives of progressive Christians. Again, the purpose of the stories is not to accuse or label anyone as racist. I do, however, wish to emphasize that people can have biases without recognizing them as racist or classist tendencies. A continual integrated experience with Jesus allows you to do the hard work of seeing people the way God intended – non-judgmentally. Matthew 7:3-5 (NIV) says,

"Why do you look at the speck of sawdust in your brother's eye and pay no attention to the plank in your own eye? How can you say to your brother, 'Let me take the speck out of your eye,' when all the time there is a plank in your own eye? You hypocrite, first take the plank out of your own eye, and then you will see clearly to remove the speck from your brother's eye."

In removing your plank, you may be less likely to judge people based on a certain stereotype or level of perfection no one can achieve without grace and mercy. We are all striving. Everyone has work to do. Everyone must do a level of soul searching that is uncomfortable.

Eventually, I moved across the hall from my new friend, Ade. I also started to meet other ministers and leaders in the community. Unsure of myself and my direction at this point I started writing. I am naturally gifted in writing but never took it seriously. I referred to my first published article 'Master Plan:' more bad news for the urban poor in chapter three. I was so proud of myself. Someone else believed my thoughts, ideas and writing were of importance.

On August 30, 2011, I received an email from a leader in the community with the subject line stating, "An exciting opportunity." I opened the email with expectancy. The email read:

Hello Angela,

I read through your Baptist Press article again yesterday - this thought came to me - why not ask Angela to work with me on the book? I've been thinking about it. I am attaching my last essay which I think can be the outline for a little book with the same title. ...I would do an introduction and have a closing section. Perhaps we could both start expanding on the basic concept of each part and then get together and meld our thoughts together. I have a publisher who is waiting for an outline proposal - but maybe you could publish it. I have lots of things bouncing around in my head, let me know what you think. Grace and Peace.

To this offer, I replied:

I think that this is a wonderful idea. I would love to work on a book with you. Let me play around with some ideas for the book and get back to you. Thank you so much for this opportunity.

I was honored at the thought of creating a book with such a great leader. It was one of the most profound moments of my life. I received a great achievement, accolades, and validation all in one day. I thought, Lord I have found my purpose.

For the next three years of my life, I pieced together a book on community ministry. I took our words and mingled them together to create an insightful book of coming together. The manuscript was complete. I printed a copy of the manuscript and we met over coffee. We discussed everything; then I created a contract.

Days later, when I did not hear from him, I called him up. To my surprise, he had invited a colleague to read the manuscript. The colleague believed the book to be a goldmine. Once the thoughts of riches entered the conversation, things changed.

"Well, if this book makes millions, I don't know if I want to be tied to YOU like that," was stated sternly through the telephone. I remember the traffic slowing down as I felt the world stop. Feeling my trauma, the statement was quickly followed by, "I am signing the contract."

I received a call later that day asking to meet at a local food court with a declaration that the contract was executed, and I was to pick it up the next afternoon. A contract modification was mentioned – my name had to be a few points smaller on the cover. I agreed.

I felt in my spirit, the meeting was not going to end well. I did not sleep at all that night nor could I eat in the morning. I drove 40 miles per hour in a 70 miles per hour zone enroute to the meeting. I reached the food court and sat in my car for fifteen minutes just praying that God would do something miraculous at this meeting. I walked in – finally – to see two people sitting at the table. This was peculiar as I have never interacted with the other person on a professional level. I have seen the other person twice throughout my five years of knowing my co-author and three years of working on the book.

The chuckles began as I walked over to the table. "You wrote the book contract too good. A lot better than I thought. I have something else in mind." I was presented with a piece of paper from an inside jacket pocket with roughly four sentences on it. It stated, **you are no longer co-author but a contributing editor for the book. You will not receive any royalties from said book. The monies paid through your previous chaplaincy work will serve as payment as the contributing editor. Signature.**

I rebuked the new contract and stated my position. The other person's reaction was shocking as they were viscerally upset because I did not back down. The acquaintance was adamant about the position as a contributing editor. After a bit of talking, I walked away from the table.

I told everyone who had ears that knew us. No one would help me.

I dedicated three years of my life to the book to have it taken in less than 20 minutes. Finally, a classmate gave me $400 to get a lawyer. The lawyer in Peachtree City, Georgia did not take me seriously and offered to write a letter for $400. With no other options, I paid her.

With that, he returned to me a letter from his lawyer dissolving the book. I was disappointed by the outcome but more so by the character of my co-author. I had confided personal things about my brother's death and spent Christmas with their family. I never saw this coming. Now I am back at square one. Meanwhile, my co-author was booking events and sharing the contents of "our" book.

I was bamboozled! I looked at the art of writing a book with this well-respected person as a measure of adding value to me. I perceived their value but not my own. The glare of validation blinded me. If you do not know your worth, you may be subject to the person that sees your value, but uses your perception against you. My perception of me led me to limit my view of my worth and awesomeness.

If you make a person feel like they made you, that person will also feel like they can break you. I was so bitter, upset, then enraged. How could this person I trusted do this to me? More upsetting were mutual acquaintances saying how sad the co-author looked. "Angela, they are really distraught and so sad about what happened." Really?!? Sad that I did not allow them to publish a manuscript I spent three years writing and editing? Feel free to insert your own brand of expletives on this line.

The bitterness of betrayal is one of the heartiest poisons that grow in the human spirit.[90] I prayed for harm to come to them. Do you know how venomous you must be to pray *to the Lord* for the Lord to stop someone's heart? My trust and my heart were broken, so Lord please take their heart. It was a tradeoff. A heart for a heart.

At that time, the Lord gave me a promise that I was too bitter to receive. I was meditating in my vehicle in front of my apartment building. I needed a moment to gather the energy to walk up the stairs leading to my apartment. The words came to me so clearly. I will give you wealth and no man will be able to take credit for it. I rested in God's word for a few minutes then exited the car.

I entered my apartment, looked at the newly dissolved manuscript and God's promise floated to the back of my mind. The flavor of bitterness returned to my mouth. I could not focus on anything but my anger. I remained bitter and disappointed about the unpublished book. Undoubtedly, God can use someone's shortcomings to allow you to become stronger. The Lord also uses people and things to get you back in line with your purpose. I knew I had to forgive the situation because it was affecting my purpose. A part of me vowed to succeed to show "them" up and that mentality took away from my working for God. It was, now, "time to grow through it" as my friend and forever Pastor Dr. Billie Boyd Cox would say.

If I am honest, I was insecure about my talent. I was easily manipulated because I needed validation. Like Moses, I thought I needed an Aaron to accompany me. I did not believe I could be successful by myself. That mindset started long before "the book." Every dream or assignment up until this point, I tried to take someone with me. I am timid by nature.

I asked God to choose someone else for this ministry on numerous occasions. I felt like my purpose was too big for me. So, before I could forgive anyone, I had to forgive myself.

I surrendered to God all of the negative things I was taught to believe about myself. I surrendered my need for validation. I asked God to forgive me for not trusting that I would be equipped and strengthened with what I needed to achieve my purpose. I asked God to release me to do his will without holding grudges.

In *the Sermon on the Plain*, Jesus addresses the crowd and pronounces the blessings and the woes. Jesus followed the blessings and woes by declaring we love our enemies. Luke 6:28 says pray for those who spitefully use you. This is also where Jesus famously instructs the crowd to turn the other cheek. We are called to forgive because As Howard Thurman put it, "hatred destroys finally the core of the life of the hater."[91] In life, you cannot simply treat people the way they treat you. Someone must have integrity.

"Do to others as you would have them do to you." Luke 6:31 (NIV)

Non-forgiveness makes you toxic to the world around you. It is like carrying around mistrust – suspicious of everything and everyone. I did not want to be toxic anymore! I made the decision to change and heal.

I needed to forgive, learn the lesson, and move forward. God's mercy and forgiveness of humanity has nothing to do with making us remember all the things God has forgiven us for. I did not want to keep a record of it or allow the painful memories to become my looking glass.

It did not happen overnight. I wish it were that simple. There are steps you must go through to reach the apex of forgiveness. I had to find myself again. I had to go back to why the Lord opened a door for me to go to seminary. Why did I move to South Carolina? I needed to hear God's voice and reconnect with my purpose. In a private event where Lonnie Allgood gave an impassioned speech about his trials and triumphs; he stated, "The two most important dates in your life is the date you were born and the date you find out your purpose for being born."

God's plan started in eternity when God chose me according to my purpose. I was formed in the image of God to be used as a vessel for that purpose. I was predestined and created for this time. Most people believe their purpose in life begins when they gain an understanding of the gift they must share with the world. They may believe it begins when they respond to the call. That is not where it begins.

God created the plan before I knew my purpose. God knew me before I was born. After I became aware of my calling, i.e. purpose for which I have individual gifts to fulfill, God declared me fit to accomplish the mission. In short, **I am literally built for this.** I realized I have all the blessings and favor needed to accomplish my purpose.

Our purpose is different from the roles we play. We are mothers, fathers, daughters, sons, wives, husbands, and caregivers. These are roles we play inside our relationships. Outside of these roles, what else are we purposed to be? We are charged with many responsibilities that call our attention to other people and things. We are so accommodating and adjust to whatever the situation requires. Hence, it is easy for us to lose ourselves. We often care for the needs of others to the point of ignoring our own needs. In doing this, we essentially relegate God's divine purpose for us. We bury it and use our gifts privately. What are you passionate about? What comes naturally to you? Are there things that happened in your life which you can connect the dots to up until this point?

To rediscover my purpose, I scheduled some time in my day when I could get quiet with no interruptions. It did not have to be a long time, but it was ours – mine and God's. I read the Bible, wrote, listened to inspirational songs, meditated, cried, and gave thanks. I reminded myself to meditate on all the good things that are going on in my life despite the uncertainties and struggles.

We give our trials and tribulation way too much time. I thought about all of the times God answered my prayers and the miracles I have seen in my life. Not to mention the many times God protected, guided, fought my battles, and pulled me out of treacherous situations.

Lastly, I meditated on how forgiving God is and how much he really does love me. In refocusing on God, I leaned on Jeremiah 29:11 and Psalm 137 – believe it or not. I had hung my harp. I had lost the song of my heart and soul. I had forgotten the songs of Zion. "How can {I} sing the songs of the Lord while in {this} foreign {place}?" (Psalm 137:4 NIV) I wanted God to teach me how to sing songs with joy while in distress. I felt exiled spiritually, mentally, and emotionally. I needed God to provide a way out so I could return to a place of God presence. In the presence of God, there is reconciliation, redemption and forgiveness. I would follow Psalm 137 with "For I know the plans that I have for you,' declares the Lord, 'plans to prosper and not harm you; plans to give you hope and a future." (Jeremiah 29:11 NIV)

I also recited Romans 8:28 NIV, "And we know that in all things God works for the good of those who love him, who have been called according to his purpose," with the understanding, that not all things feel good.

Things happen and will continue to happen in this life. We give meaning to the things that happen. However, not all the things that we deem as good are good for us and not everything we think of as bad are actually bad. We know God can turn any situation into something positive. God does this for two reasons: Our good and His glory. In times of suffering and trial I need not quit or throw up my hands because I know that God is at work in the world and God's plan is perfect.

God assures us that the difficulties of life are working for us and not against us. If God be for us, who could be against us? We need to enter each new day realizing God is for us despite obstacles and hardships. The Lord is closer to us when we go through the difficulties of life. Furthermore, He gives us the power to conquer. We are "more than conquerors," literally, through Jesus Christ! Romans 8:31-39 (NIV) This security in Christ is an absolute fact.

Once I took a few steps back and re-read the unpublished book, I laughed. I had taken on my co-author's voice and wrote a book based on that perspective. Sure, I was committed to my writing, but my writing framed their voice. The unpublished book was not the message God wanted me to preach. Suddenly, I realized that I had taken my eyes off God when writing the book. I equated victory with "that person" and not God.

Fully understanding the flawless nature of God's plan and purpose for my life, I knew my purpose was still intact, undamaged, unbroken, complete, and unharmed. I cannot and did not mess it up. I cannot get it wrong. My purpose is still fully intact AND NOTHING OR NO ONE CAN TAKE IT AWAY FROM ME!

The biggest problem I unearthed when reconnecting to my purpose was that I aimed too low in life. I altered my hopes and expectations to conform to the perception and/or cynicism of my environment. In taking steps to now forgive, I started to break free spiritually, mentally, physically, and emotionally.

I sat on the couch and opened an earlier manuscript titled, *I'm Perfectly Different.*

Chapter 5

Fifty Shades of Race: I'm Perfectly Different

"Everyone is created differently Laraina.
Our differences are what make us special."

Angela Fields

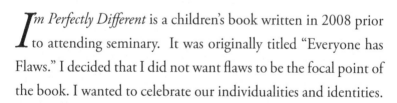

*I*m *Perfectly Different* is a children's book written in 2008 prior to attending seminary. It was originally titled "Everyone has Flaws." I decided that I did not want flaws to be the focal point of the book. I wanted to celebrate our individualities and identities.

I'm Perfectly Different is a story about a little girl and her friends learning to embrace their differences. It laid the foundation for loving yourself and helping others embrace their full selves. The main character, Laraina, learns she is different from everyone else and reacts negatively. Something different was happening to Laraina and she internalized it and believed it made her less than everyone else. Laraina is me and so many people I meet. I used *I'm Perfectly Different* to tell our collective story. I knew I needed to tell this story in hopes of helping others rewrite theirs.

However, revisiting *I'm Perfectly Different* at this point in my life was painful. I looked up to heaven and asked, "That's my assignment now? Really God?!?" First, at this time, I was working on regaining the love in my heart after the unpublished book ordeal. Second, I feel like an idiot in recovery for trusting so blindly – but everyone makes mistakes. Third, this is yet another wound to be opened.

In June of 2010, my older brother and confidante took his own life. About six months later, I finally visited the room where the suicide occurred. The room had been gone through by police, other family members, and friends.

I noticed a book on his bed. My brother talked to me about this book before his suicide. I opened the book to find the suicide note. Written on a notebook next to the book was a 1-800 number with the words "Bleaching Cream" scribbled under it.

Few things in this world are worse than realizing your loved one left this world without fully loving themselves. He was perfect but never embraced it. Later, I learned he was never comfortable in his dark skin.

I come from a long line of people who did not love their authentic selves. The oppression of society is passed down. It is duplicated and indoctrinated intra-racially and from social class to social class. I am one of fourteen children who are all dark-skinned and who were all teased to some degree as a child.

I was – verbally and physically – assaulted because of my dark hue. I was taught that my skin color was an abomination.

My paternal grandmother would tell my siblings and I that there was something wrong with us because we were dark. "Y'all were created behind God's back;" my grandmother would joke. She would tell my mom that her children were unclean and that is why we are dark. My grandmother, herself, was a dark brown woman. But she was about three shades brighter than me. This phenomenon is known as colorism.

Colorism is a direct result of racism. My grandmother had been conditioned to hate herself. She needed to find a way to feel better about herself. Her answer, subjugating someone who was a darker shade of brown. This is still a battle within communities of color to include Asian and Hispanic. Darker skinned women are viewed as less beautiful than lighter skinned women.

I was ridiculed and abused throughout my school years. On the playground, the boys would punch and kick me but were nice to the other lighter skinned little girls. I remember the point where I accepted the abuse as normal. I never felt beautiful or loved myself. It did not help that I grew up watching family members religiously sanitize their faces with bleaching creams. I struggled with the image of lightening myself and feeling inadequate.

Ironically, my mom did not wear foundation makeup. Her beauty regimen consisted of a lightening cream, eyeliner, and lipstick. I did not have anyone to talk to when it came to the issue of color, so I wrote a character named Mrs. Pleasant into

I'm Perfectly Different. I wished for a Mrs. Pleasant to talk to about my difference. I wished I could talk to someone and they could have told me it was okay. That never happened. As an adult, colorism did not change much. I drove through a toll booth and the booth operator queried, "What country are you the queen of?"

"America," I answered.

"I'm disappointed!" he continued.

This is a reoccurring theme. A conversation starter I hear a lot is, "what part of Africa are you from?"

The notion of being African American with dark skin is not good enough unless you can qualify it by being a direct descendant of the continent of Africa. Africa is home to gorgeous women but there is a grand generalization being made about a continent based on a single color. I want others to understand the implications of that belief. Colorism is another way of cherry picking and segmenting people based on pigment. Racism and colorism are so efficient that dark skin is rejected globally, furthermore, conditioning darker skinned people to hate themselves. I watch people marry or have children with lighter skinned partners, some from other races, to prevent their children from enduring the "punishment and pain" of living life as a darker skinned person.

I live between two worlds where I am twice orphaned by the racial identity given to me. I am neither fully accepted as an American nor fully embraced by the diverse culture and traditions of Africa. There is a disdain and disconnect for me proverbially as a hybrid of Africa and America. Both have been trained to believe a false narrative of who I am portrayed to be.

So, I lived a life believing that I was less than everyone else. I lived with the psychological and psychosocial effects for years. I did not know what giving or receiving love looked like.

Furthermore, suicide was something I heard little about growing up. But now every other day, suicide is affecting someone. Depression, risqué behavior, and negative coping skills are beginning earlier and earlier. Five-year olds are cutting themselves for a host of reasons. With *I'm Perfectly Different* in hand, all of these memories hovered in my mind. I knew I had to face my own insecurities and help others in the process. I had to bare my soul, becoming vulnerable, and open myself up to the ridicule once again.

A professor, early in my career, once told me I had managed to walk alongside the conveyor belt of life without ever getting on. I did live on the outskirts of life for a long time. I lived detached so that life could not hurt me anymore. Now, I had a chance to help other people not live into a lie that they were not good enough. The lies of the enemy cannot cancel out what the Lord has said. What the Lord says is we are more than conquerors. I can do anything through Christ who gives me strength. (Romans 8:37 & Philippians 4:13)

I wanted to know how I would begin but I knew the answer to how was yes. I did not know how to publish a book, nor did I have the resources. So, I turned the manuscript into a PowerPoint presentation and started calling random places asking if I can read my book. I started my journey with a laptop, mini projector, and a PowerPoint presentation of *I'm Perfectly Different.*

Now, for all of you who work, have, or live around children, you understand that children tell you exactly what is on their minds. I set out to read *I'm Perfectly Different* to children from the South to the Northeast.

Those children tore me to shreds. Preschoolers and kindergarteners were the worst.

"Why is your face spiky right there?" **Because I was blessed with facial hair.**

"You have white hair!" **White hair runs in my family!**

"Your teeth are a little crooked." **I know. I love my crooked teeth and smiling.**

I had to account for every imperfection, whether I was ready or not.

One preschooler yelled from the back, "I know what color I am. I'm gold!"

Here we go… I tried to curtail the conversation because I knew what was coming.

Everyone is made differently, I reiterated. Different does not only mean color.

It was too late.

The other children began blurting out their color. Again, I tried to shift the conversation to other differences. But the little boy in the back would not quit. He made an observation that he needed everyone to know. **"I know what color you are; you are black."**

I exhaled and said, "Yes, I am a darker-skinned woman. I deserve to be loved and valued no matter my difference from your golden complexion. We are all beautiful."

I talked to honest child after brutally honest child day after day, month after month. I learned to listen to the children's honesty, but I refused to internalize it. I accepted it as a gift from God.

Then something else happened. Adults who heard the story and attended the workshops identified with the book. I was constantly approached by adults who were suffering from the lasting effects of bullying, sense of worthlessness, overcompensating for different characteristics, and poor social and emotional support.

Words can live and take on a life of their own. Using the wrong words hurt others and the effects can be lasting. As a result, individuals' personal lives deteriorate.

As I toured the northeast and south with, *I'm Perfectly Different* I realized more was needed to reinforce the message to others who were struggling with a multitude of things. I created a basic curriculum that taught love, self-realization, and coping strategies to people of all ages.

I wanted to change the culture by interjecting new measures and understanding of love. Part one through three of the curriculum covered the pedagogy of love as demonstrated by God, self-realization, and the development of empathy or compassion for others.

Pedagogy of love

We are rapidly moving toward a society that celebrates intolerance, violence, and unforgiveness. There is no longer a powerful discourse on the benefits of love. Love is crucial in developing one's self-esteem and creating a well-proportioned life. Love does no harm and cares for one another. The absence of a sustained focus on love is a failure to acknowledge the needs of the spirit. The pedagogy of love is the method of teaching love. It examines our thoughts about love. On the epithelial or surface level, the lack of love appears to be a lack of respect. A lack of respect resembles coarseness toward others and a crudeness toward someone's feelings or well-being. At the core, however, there is a lack of love for themselves resulting in a lack of empathy for anyone else.

Love flows out of our beliefs, thinking, and values – out of the totality of who we are. It is what you see, hear, and are taught. If you learn to hate yourself, you will hate yourself. And if you hate yourself, how can you love someone else? It is not possible.

The first question I ask when I discuss, *I'm Perfectly Different* is what does love look like?

I convey that love is not always "me first." Love does not hit, love does not force itself on others, love does not take pleasure in gossip or rumors. Love does not watch or join in abuse and bullying.

Love does no wrong to others. Love is not lessening who you are to fit a mold that is abusive to you. You do not have to look far for love. Your very existence is love.

Self-realization

Self-realization is getting to the center of who you are without self-imposed barriers. Self-realization dovetails the pedagogy of love. It covers loving and embracing yourself and your individuality. It reinforces the value of one's own life and the lives of others. It explores the dangers of comparing one's self to others and humanities inability to live up to ever changing standards. Self-realization will essentially renew one's value by embracing the power of 'you'.

The ultimate myth is to assimilate to the dominant culture believing you are going to be looked upon differently. You will never be viewed as the same and you are losing your identity in the process. Respect yourself. What defines you is not resembling the crowd but differing from the crowd. You cannot live into other people standards. Standards change and there is no guarantee if you change, you will be accepted. How far are you willing to go to assimilate?

Coping strategies

Coping strategies serve to teach individuals to become aware of their emotions. It highlights thinking through emotions and not be controlled by emotions alone. It explores an individual's impulsive reactions based on emotion and the dire consequences. This is critical and complex especially if you are not aware of your triggers and you are still working on loving yourself. "A holistic view of the human experience holds thought and emotion together. The emotion, then, becomes vital in what we do, how we think, and how we understand."[92]

Emotion is referred to as feelings and its distinctive thoughts, psychological and biological states, and the range of propensities to act. [93] A study of criminals showed a characteristic in common – a history of emotional neglect and little opportunity for attunement.[94] Children's empathy is shaped by seeing how others react when someone is in distress. Children imitate what they see. [95] It is also shaped by experiencing a lack of attention and protection.

Coping strategies invite individuals to discuss their feelings and emotions as well as maladaptive and adaptive coping measures.

Dare to dream

Dare to dream is the final push to encourage the people to embrace a fuller more productive life. It serves as a means of exposing or reintroducing people to their dreams, goals, and ideas without the burden of assimilation or shrinking to fit.

Positive fortifications reduce and eliminate the need for validation from outside of yourself. Yes! You are important.

Yes! You are loved. Yes! Your future does not have to be a repeat of your past. You are perfectly different. Embrace it. Do not let anyone take that away from you. Society cannot make imperfect what God has rendered perfect and purposeful. In Acts 10:11-15 the Lord gives Peter a vision with a command to eat what is considered unclean by the Jews. When Peter protested, the Lord says, "Do not call something unclean if God has made it clean." This message resonated with Peter as Cornelius, a Gentile, requested Peter's presence at his home. Jews and Gentiles were forbidden from interacting due to the law of the land. In Acts of the Apostles commonly known as Acts 10:34-35 NIV, Peter began to speak: "I now realize how true it is that God does not show favoritism but accepts from every nation the one who fears him and does what is right."

Therefore, regardless of nationality, race, or other humanly constructed barrier, you were created from the ultimate source of love, purified, and made whole through the love of God. That is the Master's plan. You are made in God's image and you must know that you are lovable just the way you are. Whatever you are struggling with, God can help. Accept yourself and embrace who you are.

Through *I'm Perfectly Different*, I was able to embrace the inequity that gave others an advantage. Someone else's inequity creates an advantage for some and extreme disadvantage for others. As Dr. King wrote of educational inequity, "They are never honest enough to admit that the academic cultural lags in {disinvested} communities are themselves the result of segregation and discrimination."96

My inequity, however, is not being used as an excuse. Settling or being stagnant is not a step toward mental and emotional freedom. I just knew that I had to work harder due to inequity. As Anne Lamont says, "If you only want to know what you already know, you're dying. You are saying leave me alone; I'm comfortable in this rat hole where it is dry and warm, and no one is challenging me. But this is death. New light, new questions, new possibilities can be scary and disappointing, but it is life..." [97] I wanted to do better. I am determined to be better. Someone else can want so much for you but no one can make you want it for yourself.

I entered undergraduate school with a seventh-grade education. I scored very low on my SATs but I persisted. One of psychology's open secrets is the relative inability of grades, IQ, or SAT scores, despite their popular mystique, to predict unerringly who will succeed in life. [98] God uses ordinary people and things to accomplish a divine mission. Peter and John were ordinary, "unschooled" men who accomplished great things through Christ.

In the first letter of Paul to the Corinthians, recalling Isaiah 29:14, "I will destroy the wisdom of the wise, and the understanding of those who have understanding, I will confound." Where is the wise person? Where is the scribe? Where is the debater of this age? Has God not made foolish the wisdom of the world? (1 Corinthians 1:19-20 NASB)

God's wisdom surpasses human wisdom and is in sharp contrast to the wisdom of this world. Society relishes human wisdom. The wisdom – sophia 99– of this world teaches us to rely on our thoughts or intelligence. In fact, the word philosophy (phileo + sophia) literally means to love wisdom. However, one cannot depend on human wisdom alone. There is a godly wisdom that defies human understanding. I am a consummate learner but no longer hard on myself for not knowing. What I do not know…I learn. I once felt that I had to know everything before I took a stand, but I cannot know everything. I just stepped out of the mental cage and kept taking steps.

This new understanding frees me from the fear of elevation or having an opinion. I must be myself and love who God made me…believe differently… and I will not shrink to fit. It is a process to free my mind, but it is necessary for those coming behind you. I made up my mind that… my circumstances cannot define who God said I can become. Only I can do that.

I was so committed to *I'm Perfectly Different* and my new revelation. I forewent my home and conducted a year-long book tour while nearly homeless. This was my third, longest but final incidence of homelessness to date. For the record, I do not like being homeless.

During my book tour…I would book summer camps because they gave me a cabin for the night. I had no money and little help. I couch surfed and – when possible – stayed in cheap motels.

In the afternoons, I would be in the library or parked in the cemetery praying myself to sleep. I knew my life was not my own and I had a greater purpose. It was challenging but through the challenges I reflected on this journey toward becoming God's best.

After almost a year of touring, I did what any self-respect adult would do. I called my mom. I returned to New Jersey to live with my mom. I needed to be replenished and to regroup. Most importantly, I needed a hug and to be loved in a way only a mom can provide.

Chapter 6

No invitation, no thank you...!

If you see a problem, fix it. The answer to how is Yes.

―❧―

I moved back to my hometown of Paterson, New Jersey from the South. Moving back to Paterson was quite an adjustment. It was not the city I remembered or maybe it simply lost its sense of home. I could have also remembered Paterson more favorably as a child of the city but understood the derelict as an adult.

My mom resided in a different part of town since the last time I visited. My mom and dad were homeowners since the late 70's. When the recession of 2008 hit, my parents were divorced and living separately. During the recession, my mom ultimately lost her home and became a renter for the first time in over thirty years. My mom moved into a thinly insulated, noisy three-story home near a railroad track.

It is directly across the street from a mechanic shop that seems like it never closes. There is a bar on the corner that opens on the weekend and holidays. The music blares until 3:00 am all weekend long. There is an influx of intoxicated people on the corner until the wee hours of the morning and parking is a nightmare. Occasionally, dog owners would curb their dogs and throw trash on the sidewalk. It hardly felt like home.

I called a pastor friend of mine and vented about my mom's – and now my – current living situation. The outcome of the conversation was the revelation that people put trash where they see trash. How profound! A people group accustomed to being relegated or devalued, contribute to the trashing of their own neighborhood.

I could not help but to juxtapose the community in Paterson, New Jersey with the emancipated Israelites. The Israelites were oppressed for 400 years. That is multi-generational oppression, suppression, and poverty. They were called lazy even as they were building the nation. The constant mental, physical, and emotional degradation caused a deep indoctrination of unworthiness.

As an aside, it does not help when people from wealthier neighborhoods continually transport "problematic residents" to poor neighborhoods. For example, I have witnessed those who are homeless, suffer from addiction, and/or mental health disorder brought to densely populated urban areas and left there. It is said that these individuals are being transported to poorer neighborhoods for resources or treatment. However, resources are drained in areas where there is a high concentration of people. I believe residents of affluent neighborhoods do not like the look of visibly vulnerable populations within their community. Affluent people have an image to uphold and love to tout what is not occurring in their community. In reality, the problem is hidden or being transferred to less affluent areas. Somehow it is believed that that is where vulnerable people belong. Consequently, the idea of the reverse happening terrifies those in wealthy neighborhoods i.e. social exclusion.

In 2020, I set out to open a shelter and resource facility in one of the most affluent counties in the United States. I located a property that would have been perfect. It was very motivating because I would be able to help families affected by the pandemic and expand services. However, I was stopped by an ally, believe it or not. Vulnerable people did not belong in the area "bouncing in and out of our school system." Zoning and ordinance regulations were subsequently used to disqualify necessary services from entering a community where 'the shelter' did not belong.

People are not disposable no matter the community. But, if they are accustomed to being treated as disposable, that is a hard belief to change. It is hard to see yourself outside of the way people treat you. As a result, they became like the families in the wilderness.

Families in the wilderness or vulnerable families exist in a perpetual state of crisis, questioning, and distrust. What will we eat? What will we drink? Where will we live? How will we live? Life is, now, about survival opposed to living and thriving. Life becomes a journey to nowhere. The wilderness mindset is passed down through the generations. This is why, I believe, we have seven-year olds looking for a way out via guns and "getting this money."

In Exodus, the generations who were stuck in the oppressive mindset died after years of wandering in the wilderness. How many more people are we going to watch die in the wilderness? Furthermore, the generation that never knew oppression, mentally or otherwise, entered the Promised Land. The Promised Land is a place of abundance. It is the next level, and it is time to lead the children from the wilderness into the land of more.

Let us explore the plight of Moses and the journey to freedom. Moses was God's servant leader. Moses, once held as royalty in Egypt, fled persecution for killing a slave overlord. Moses resided in Midian for forty years after fleeing Egypt. Moses' old life was behind him and far from his mind when God commissioned him to rejoin the community he had fled forty years earlier.

Moses doubted his ability to challenge the sociopolitical system in Egypt. He also questioned his approach upon returning as Moses was wanted for murder. Moses then, asked: "Who am I going to say sent me?" This simply means, "Tell me who I can point them to when they question me?" Moses conjured the spirit of Adam and wanted someone to point to outside of himself as a point of reference.

Moses' fear did not nullify his assignment. Moses talked about his inadequacy to God and asked to send his brother Aaron in his place. God obliged Moses and sent Aaron along with him. What Moses did not understand, however, is that God was training him in Midian for four decades. Moses' job in Midian was leading the sheep in the wilderness.

The imagery of shepherding is used often in the Bible. Well-known figures in the Bible were shepherds turned prophet or community leader to include Moses and King David. Jesus is even known as the Good Shepherd. Shepherding is used figuratively to represent the relation of civil authorities to their subjects and of God to his people. The shepherd is also depicted as a responsible overseer and caretaker who tends to the flock lovingly.

1 Peter 5:2-4 says, "Be shepherds of God's flock that is under your care, watching over them—not because you must, but because you are willing, as God wants you to be; not pursuing dishonest gain, but eager to serve; not lording it over those entrusted to you, but being examples to the flock. And when the Chief Shepherd appears, you will receive the crown of glory that will never fade away."

The prophet Isaiah tells us that the shepherd "gathers the lambs in the arms and carries them close to the heart" (Isaiah 40:11 NIV). "The bond between a shepherd and the sheep has all the qualities of a true family." [100]

"Shepherding, moreover, requires going ahead of the flock to find a secure place to graze and keeping a watchful eye for predators and assuring the sheep did not stray. Often shepherds or shepherdesses had to guard the fold through the dark hours from the wily attempts of the prowling thief" (1 Samuel 17:34).[101] "Shepherding also requires a tenderness toward the young, feeble, and sometimes misdirected." [102] The connation of the sheep without a shepherd symbolizes the demoralization of individuals or nations who had forgotten

God. Demoralization is engrafted into the people causing them to lose faith in God and in their voice.

God does not waste an experience. Moses was prepared and he did not know it. Like Moses, you are ready whether you believe it or not. God heard the cries of the people and prepared Moses to shepherd his own people out of bondage.

Children are struggling under the pressures of poverty and inadequate educational opportunities. Due to systemic deficiencies, they grow into labels that become indicative of who they are. Dysfunctional, unintelligent, and lazy are labels placed on top of hard work. I can attest that even if one manages to escape the environment, the labels are championed in larger arenas."[103] The solution is to provide a level of equity for the children through education to include emotional intelligence, economics and the legal systems. "Start children off on the way they should go, and even when they are old, they will not turn from it." (Proverbs 22:6-7 NIV)

Moses' assignment as a shepherd, community activist and advocate were to represent the community on key issues and facilitate conversations designed to enlighten powerful groups on how to respond to the plight of the people. Advocates are responsible for improving communities by addressing power issues, solving conflicts, proposing improvements, setting goals, and creating positive change.[104] This measure will help the people grow out of poverty.

Community advocates mobilize the communities toward conducive efforts with the hope of creating a new community.

The new communal atmosphere allows all people to come together around a common cause and act in support of everyone's shared interests.

I had to be willing to effect change by being an example... even if it meant creating community pride by cleaning up after other people's dogs. I also began serving the homeless population in the community. I did not wait for people to invite me to the table. I sought opportunities to help and I showed up.

It is proverbial that ninety percent of success in life is just showing up. Show up and keep showing up. This is especially true in building trust within a community. Trust is not developed in the abstract, but in the tangible – touch and feel of human interaction.

My brother once told me that leadership starts in your relationships and relationships are cultivated through spending intentional time with another. As you move among the community building relationships, please understand that the Lord is moving with you. Take the time to build strong, genuine, and lasting relationships with people where they are.

Start small, strike up a conversation with your neighbor non-judgmentally. The power of relationship building is witnessing the needs of the people with the people. Do not wait to be invited and do not be discouraged. Be strong and courageous.

As the biblical narrative of Exodus ends, Moses learns that liberation is a slow and tireless process. I, too, understand it will take time; dedication and sacrifice to reach this goal. I understand that it will be hard to achieve without God and a vision.[105]

Now, the flip side is the people in the wilderness were damaged. They prayed and God answered their prayer with Moses. When Moses showed up, the Israelites did not applaud or show outward appreciation. Remember the people have been oppressed for 400 years. Four hundred years of oppression is difficult to change in a short period of time. Moses may have encountered attitudes like:

Who the hell are you?

What can you do for me?

Why do I need you?

Do you think you are better than us?

Moses was charged with leading the people to a place they did not know they needed.

Families may come for nourishment with frustration because the journey is arduous. As in Exodus, the Israelites probably had a different vision of freedom. As with promotion, we tend to think of the fabulousness that comes from it – more money, better home, increased travel i.e. the accoutrements. But in everything, there is always work involved. There are no short cuts. Sorry! If you need a moment to cry, I will wait. 3…2…1…Okay, back to freedom.

Freedom is not just physical but mental, spiritual, and emotional. The Israelites gained physical freedom, but their minds were still captive. The centuries of being beaten physically, mentally, emotionally, and spiritually takes a toll.

Maslow's Hierarchy of Needs is a theory in psychology that is centered on human needs and motivation. It is an eight-tier model that includes: physiological needs, safety, love and belonging, esteem, cognitive, and aesthetic needs, self-actualization, and transcendence.[106]

See Model Below

Deficiencies

1. *Physiological needs* - air, food, drink, shelter, warmth, sleep.

2. *Safety needs* - protection from elements, security, order, law, stability, freedom from fear.

3. *Love and belongingness needs* - friendship, intimacy, trust, and acceptance, receiving and giving affection and love. Affiliating, being part of a group (family, friends, work).

4. *Esteem needs* - which Maslow classified into two categories: (i) esteem for oneself (dignity, achievement, mastery, independence) and (ii) the desire for reputation or respect from others (e.g., status, prestige).

Growth

5. *Cognitive needs* - knowledge and understanding, curiosity, exploration, need for meaning and predictability.

6. *Aesthetic needs* - appreciation and search for beauty, balance, form, etc.

7. *Self-actualization needs* - realizing personal potential, self-fulfillment, seeking personal growth and peak experiences.[107]

8. *Transcendence needs* - A person is motivated by values which transcend the personal self (e.g., service to others, the pursuit of science, religious faith).[108]

At the most basic level, Maslow's Hierarchy of Needs declares that your basic needs must be fulfilled before you are motivated to grow. "When a deficit need has been 'more or less' satisfied it will go away, and our activities become habitually directed towards meeting the next set of needs that we have yet to satisfy."[109] It is important to say that some processes are on-going. Also, people do not always start at number one and can bounce between a few needs.

The point is, sometimes, vulnerable families and individuals have needs that must be met before you can help them help themselves. Therefore, after Moses freed the Israelites, they grumbled against him. They also wanted to go back to bondage when things got hard. This is classic Stockholm Syndrome. Stockholm syndrome is an emotional attachment to a captor formed by a hostage because of continuous stress, dependence, and a need to cooperate for survival.[110] Even when something higher is calling the people to freedom, they do not believe that they can be free. As a result, some of the people God called Moses to free almost behaved like the system God called Moses to confront.

The people may grumble but they just want to be heard. Better yet…the people want to be loved and feel supported.

Let us not forget the transformation or everyone favorite word **change** that is occurring. Change is uncomfortable for anybody. The pain in the familiar can seem better than the pain of change.

Lead them out anyway. Lead them into the promise. Children are looking for a way out without God. God was the way out for the Israelites and God is the way out for us today. Be their way out beyond the wilderness. Not as a savior... we have Jesus for that. But as one who shepherds. So, what was the outcome of the formerly enslaved people? An imperfect people group becomes stronger and self-sustaining. The next generation will be able to fight the good fight of social standing and equality in the new land.

Do not worry about being appreciated. God will send you moments of thanks when it is needed. Take your position. We have the power to transform lives and communities. The idea of a better hopeful and loving community is just an abstract concept until we see it manifested in some neighbors who believe it is possible.[111]

Chapter 7

Taking the lead

"If your Presence does not go with us, do not send us up from here."

Exodus 33:15 NIV

B eing out front is not natural to me as I am an introvert. In fact, quarantining during Covid-19 has not been hard for me at all. I am naturally reserved and private. So, taking the lead was hard for me to grasp.

Facing the 'crowd' is mentally, spiritually, and emotionally draining without the added scrutiny. Leaders endure more criticism than anyone else. Your responsibility and accountability levels increase with the scrutiny and your faults will be held under a microscope. Like the children from the reading of *I'm Perfectly Different*, people will pick you apart but for more malicious reasons. And some criticism is wrapped in standards and is nothing personal.

I remember my first pastorate internship; I was told of the requirement of women in ministry that they should not show their shoulders on the pulpit and that lap guards are a must. Lap guards, for those who are not familiar, are elongated scarves women place on their legs when sitting in a skirt. Lap guards help to keep wondering eyes focused on God instead of feminine body parts. Therefore, I decided to wear a black robe from my neck to my ankles. But someone noticed my shoes. I, then, carried a reference about my shoes. A congregant labeled me as the minister with 'those' high heel shoes. Guilty! I love a good heel.

In accepting criticism and scrutiny from the crowd, I know I am in good company. Charles H. Spurgeon was one of the most prolific preachers in England during the 19th century. Spurgeon doggedly preached the gospel of Jesus Christ. At the core of his ministry was a universal and exemplary example of Christian virtue. However, you may be surprised to learn that he suffered from bouts of depression that worsened with intense scrutiny over his sermons. He persevered and his sermons are still among the most quoted in theological circles. However, the voices of the scrutinizing crowd do not make history. You will read some of Charles Spurgeon's words later in this chapter.

Additionally, the years of being told I was not good enough had taken their toll. For example, after graduate school, I was gently told by the coordinator charged with referring me to pastoral positions in South Carolina that certain congregations were not <u>ready</u> for an African American female pastor. The exact wording included "they would not take you seriously as an African American person or as a woman pastor."

I am a hardworking, dedicated, non-threatening woman with a Master of Divinity from an accredited university with a 3.6 GPA and all I want to do is serve. However, two of the three uncontrollable things in my life at birth nullified my fitness for the position I was credentialled for – my race and my sex. I sure hope things have changed since 2012.

Nevertheless, devastated – and feeling the impact of that conversation – I went to a ministry acquaintance to discuss the assessment. Nearly in tears, I repeated the words back to my confidante who is an African American male. To my surprise, he concurred and added, "And you are *really* black too." This meant that a black woman with a richer skin tone is less likely to be seriously considered as a leader among non-minorities or antiquated men with superficial beliefs, respectively.

Therefore, taking the lead and speaking in front of people or having a huge engagement to attend gives me anxiety weeks in advance. I thank God that I can relate to Jesus as an introvert. The Pharisees, Sadducees, and the multitude were draining Jesus mentally, physically, and spiritually. This is my interpretation, of course. Jesus was called to do the work of the Father but repeatedly withdrew – sending everyone away – to pray and draw strength from God. For me, pulling away from the crowd to reflect and pray is essential for Christian leadership.

Christian leadership, or any type of leadership, is not lordship. Leadership is not about the size of your following. It is about the quality of the leadership that matters. Leadership raises the vision, values, and aspirations of both the leader and the follower to new levels of expectation. A leader exercises leadership by attempting to make a positive difference in the lives of those around them.

Leadership that flows out of insecurity and self-need is not leadership at all. Christian "leadership requires the ability to look beyond the narrow confines of one's own life, into someone else's situation and want for them the same things we want for ourselves." [112]

Leading people requires a quality of character and a credibility worth trusting. Leadership, for me, requires the Holy Spirit and a healthy dependence on God so I will not become puffed up enough to believe I am God. Some of the clearest illustrations of ineffective leadership in the bible are in 1 Kings. The Book of 1 Kings outlines the reign of rulers, good and bad, over the Israelites. Although, the leaders did not have the Holy Spirit, they did have clear instructions from the prophets. Examples of poor leaders outlined in 1 Kings are monarchs who appointed erroneous or unqualified people to high places like Jeroboam in 1 Kings 13:33-34 (NIV). Monarchs also lead the people astray by using falsehoods and man-made idols like Ahab in 1 Kings chapters 16-22. Faulty leaders, furthermore, did not heed the wisdom of the elders or people with experience like Rehoboam in 1 Kings 12. In short, if the leader is not sensible, it taints the people. It also repeats a cycle of victimizing the people you are purposed to serve.

In *Transforming Power: Biblical Strategies for Making a Difference in Your Community*, Robert Linthicum states that there are two kinds of leadership power. The first is unilateral power in which persons and systems control others from the top. Unilateral power is dominating. "Dominating power is exercised by government or groups through the force of guns and physical intimidation. Many in different institutions and communities face injustice, crime, poverty, and racism due to political, social, and economic evils contained within these power structures. The power of the world's evil is far greater than the sins of its individuals." [113]

The second is Relational power. Relational power is biblical and non-oppressive. It consists of mutual and reciprocal powers. This is where people come together to accomplish things that make the community and the world a better place. Relational power is what Jesus promised to give us as we connect with all the people to discover what needs to be done. Unilateral power tends to bring instability, fear, and discouragement. Relational power brings confidence, stability, and hope for a better shared future. "Political, social, and economic systems will use power either destructively or constructively. As people of God, we will either have to confront the abuse of power or affirm its use." [114]

Faith leaders have not responded effectively to the systemic abuse of power. However, throughout the Bible, God has empowered the people to stand up to injustice especially relating to the poor and oppressed. My work is not about me or how I feel.

Initially, rejection and fear caused me to hide my light. Then, one night in bed, I dreamt I was a bright lamp overrun by cobwebs. I am not talking about any ordinary cobwebs. I am talking about the old, dusty cobwebs that even the spiders abandoned. I felt like I was in the dream for a long time. Just me, looking at myself as a lamp dripping in cobwebs. The cobwebs just surrounding the light and made the room feel dull and damp. It was very distressing. Matthew 5:15 NLT says, "No one lights a lamp and then puts it under a basket. Instead, a lamp is placed on a stand, where it gives light to everyone in the house." I received God's message loud and clear.

As a leader, I need to be a beacon of light to the world. I want, also, to train others to be the light. Leaders do not lead in perpetuity. There comes a time when God calls for a new beginning with new leadership.

I am called to stand with the people and uphold a holy agenda. The ways in which I will accomplish the agenda have not been wholly revealed but believing that the answer to how is always yes, I am taking the lead with a divine purpose of servitude, advocacy, and sacrifice. Servitude is true leadership. I will not despise the small places. As a leader, I will appreciate others' worth and realize that I am not above any job. I will not enable the people but encourage and empower them. Jesus was meek when he needed to be and radical when necessary. Jesus wept with friends and endured pain with and for the people. Jesus was, is, and forever will be, the light of the world.

Furthermore, the light knows what lies hidden in darkness. We must learn to be the light amid a toxic environment wherever it may be. It may make people uncomfortable because you are a reminder of their darkness. Lighting the world means changing the culture. And here is the thing. The plot to kill Jesus did not end when Christ was crucified. Jesus' crucifiers also sought to kill the testimony associated with the true power of God. Therefore, I will remain the light in dark places by drawing strength from the Spirit of God in the face of my crucifers.

There is a poem by Marianne Williamson called "*Our Deepest Fear.*" *Our Deepest Fear* states that we should not be afraid of the power within ourselves. We should in fact, be strong, bold, and brave. "…And as we let our light shine, we unconsciously or without knowing it, give other people permission to let their light shine."[115]

Understanding this, I know that there is no waiting until I am **ready** to take the lead. In leadership, what is ready? How does one get ready? In my experience, one gets 'ready' for leadership by leading – committing to the act. Furthermore, few people in the Bible had the luxury of feeling ready for an assignment.

I love how Dr. King chronicled his journey to leadership in *Stride Toward Freedom*. Dr. King received an education but had never led a movement when he was catapulted into leading what became known as the Civil Rights Movement. He stepped up, sought guidance from other leaders, and allowed himself to be used for a higher purpose. Dr. Martin Luther King, Jr. tackled Civil Rights in a way that allowed God to get through to the masses. However, King did it in a way that did not play into the savagery of black people. The savage nature of the dominant culture was revealed, and the love of Christ was seen through him.

I am just a vessel. I am nothing. God is everything. It is not about me. Leaders cannot hide. As Reverend Dr. Billie Boyd Cox says, "Leaders need to be seen leading." This is what I try to put into practice.

When the pressures of leading arise, I will not be consumed. I repeat 2 Corinthians 4:8-9, "we are hard pressured on every side, but not crushed, perplexed, but not in despair; persecuted, but not abandoned; struck down, but not destroyed." I pray and ask God for guidance when I am tempted to succumb to the scrutiny of being the light. I am not perfect, and I am not expected to be perfect. There are moments when I want to retaliate or quit. There are times when the Spirit of Pettiness would like to break through and straighten out a soul or two. But I resist and I do not quit. Leaders do not quit or retaliate (much). Leaders go through trouble…we vent, we cry, we exercise, we name golf balls as we hit them, but we pray and keep going.

Fear and anxieties must fall into perspective. I am in God's hands. I cannot focus my energy so much on the scrutiny or the battles I will face. I choose to stay focused on the One who is with me – guiding me and fighting for me.

The flipside, nevertheless, is remaining humble. There are always two sides of a coin. I cannot become proud imagining how great I am yet to be. Humility involves a continuous relationship with God. I am not prepared to tell anyone that I have this figured out. I could remember as I was writing the unpublished book, I started feeling myself. I sashayed into a room and did a two-finger wave to the people in the room. I was published, winning awards, and writing what I believed was a game changing book. God humbled me quickly. The bigger the platform, the bigger the prayers to keep me grounded and surrounded by the right people. I know that God opposes the proud but honors humility.

To avoid making the mistakes of the above chapters i.e. ownership and needing validation, I ruminate on Micah 6:8 which says, "But he's already made it plain how to live, what to do, what GOD is looking for in men and women. It's quite simple: Do what is fair and just to your neighbor, be compassionate and loyal in your love, and don't take yourself too seriously— take God seriously." The New International Version states it another way. It says, "He has shown you, O mortal, what is good. And what does the LORD require of you? To act justly and to love mercy and to walk humbly with your God."

In his sermon, *Walk humbly with thy God*, Charles Spurgeon says, "…Dare to keep with God, dare to have him as your daily Friend, be bold enough to come to him who is within the veil, talk with him, walk with him, as a man walks; with his familiar friend; but walk humbly with him." [116]

In the sermon, Charles continues to say,

"The way to the top is downstairs; sink yourself into the highest place. If I am puffed up, God is sinking. It is inconceivable to walk proudly with God. Those in God's kingdom turn the world's values upside down. If you want to live for God, you must be ready to say and do what seems strange to the world. You must be willing to give when others take, to love when others hate, to help where others have abused." [117]

I urge fellow leaders not to lose this perspective because it is too easy to lord over and oppress others. Seek first the kingdom of God. "Do nothing out of selfish ambition or vain conceit. Rather in humility value others above yourselves, not looking to your own interests but each of you to the interests of the others." Philippians 2:3-4 (NIV)

Let me reiterate, taking the lead cannot be about things like money, cars, homes, or clout. "Shepherds who feed only themselves... are {like} clouds without rain, blown along by the wind; autumn trees, without fruit and uprooted—twice dead." Jude 1:12b (NIV)

Far too often, our possessions are seen as the fruit of our tree. The type of car we drive, how much money we make, the houses we own, and whether we adorn the latest and greatest fashions are factored into our "reaping a harvest." We, however, must be careful not to believe that cars, clothes, and money are fruits of the vine. If you lose your home, your money, and your car; would you still be able to produce fruit? If you are called to stand for something that may jeopardize your finances, would you stand?

Whatever blessings are received is extra. Acquiring nice things is not the goal but bearing fruit is. John 15:1-2 NIV says, "I am the true vine, and my Father is the gardener. He cuts off every branch in me that bears no fruit, while every branch that does bear fruit, he prunes so that it will be even more fruitful."

Fruit is an edible part of a plant that harvest seeds which are implanted into fertile ground for the purpose of reproducing a harvest. Our lives should resemble the attractive, nurturing nature of a fruit. The people around us should be able to take the fruit of our branches, digest it and replant the seed in new places.

To be completely transparent, both I and the other author of the unpublished book took our eyes off God. I was focused on acclaim and he was focused on the money. In return, God promptly snatched the book. The purpose of God's blessing is found in 2 Corinthians 9:10-13 which says,

> Now he who supplies seed to the sower and bread for food will also supply and increase your store of seed and will enlarge the harvest of your righteousness. You will be enriched in every way so that you can be generous on every occasion, and through us your generosity will result in thanksgiving to God. This service that you perform is not only supplying the needs of the Lord's people but is also overflowing in many expressions of thanks to God. Because of the service by which you have proved yourselves, others will praise God for the obedience that accompanies your confession of the gospel of Christ, and for your generosity in sharing with them and with everyone else.

One more thing I learned about taking the lead – is preparing for promotion. God gives promotion by showing us the work that needs to be done. In Joshua 1, Joshua was installed as a leader. Immediately, Joshua was commissioned to lead the Israelites into the "Promised Land" after 40 years of wandering in the desert. However, another battle was taking place across the Jordan River and it was attached to the "promotion." I know what you are thinking. This does not sound like our idea of a promotion. But godly promotion often means increased responsibility and a new battle.

God commissioned Joshua to do three things: (1) to lead the people into the Promised Land, (2) to defeat the enemies of the land, and (3) to claim their inheritance. (Joshua 1:1-6 NIV) Joshua may have discovered that to whom much is given, much is required. Luke 12:48 (ESV)

Furthermore, Joshua was told to obey the word of God and be strong and courageous. (Joshua 1:7-9) God did not give Joshua a detailed explanation as to how he would accomplish his assignment. Joshua was expected to believe in the promises of God opposed to explanations.

God promises Joshua that every place his foot treads will be given unto them: "I will give it to your descendants." In the Hebrew language, "every place your foot should tread" is in the imperfect tense, which signifies future actions. But the verb "give" or *nātan* is in perfect tense which signifies past events or actions. Hence, every future place you should tread is yours.

This verse in context tells us that before you even started to walk in your assignment, God has already given you the victory. But, work is required. Trust God's promises and step out by faith. The Lord will give you the directions you need when you need them.

Things are falling apart in our communities, God is calling us to lead by standing, standing for, standing with, and standing up for without distractions. In times of chaos and unrest in our nation, God is calling people to move beyond passive listening to deter further oppression or suppression of a community; bypassing the preset barriers designed to keep us from leading and standing.

Chapter 8

We are all connected

*We are all a part of a global community rather we want
to be or not.*

❧

In Ephesians 4:1-14, the Apostle Paul writes about unity and maturity in the Body of Christ. There is a spiritual unity among Christians as the Body of Christ that supersedes any underlying unity. The Apostle Paul asks the body of Christ to "be completely humble and gentle; be patient, bearing with one another in love. Make every effort to keep the unity of the Spirit through the bond of peace." (Ephesians 4: 2-3NIV) The Apostle Paul continues,

> Christ himself gave the apostles, the prophets, the evangelists, the pastors, and teachers, to equip his people for works of service, so that the body of Christ may be built up until we all reach unity in the faith and in the knowledge of the Son of God and become mature, attaining

to the whole measure of the fullness of Christ. Then we will no longer be infants, tossed back and forth by the waves, and blown here and there by every wind of teaching and by the cunning and craftiness of people in their deceitful scheming. (Ephesians 4:11-14 NIV)

In short, we are all connected first as the body of Christ – "one Lord, one faith, one baptism." (Ephesians 4:5 NIV) We are members of one family. So in Christ we, though many, form one body, and each member belongs to all the others. (Romans 12:5 NIV)

Regrettably, we are still struggling in our nation and in our communities to be hospitable to those whom we perceive to be different or unworthy while professing Christianity. Transgressions among the people "is not about the Adult bookstore on the corner; it is the hard heart, …and all the isms, racism, classism, sexism and so forth." [118] "If one part suffers, every part suffers with it; if one part is honored, every part rejoices with it." 1 Corinthians 12:26 (NIV)

In Jesus' parable of the Good Samaritan, Jesus talks about a man who had been accosted by thieves, who robbed and beat him, leaving him near death on the roadside. Two travelers on the road see the man and his predicament but pass by on the other side. The plot of the story thickens considerably when Jesus introduces the next person on the road, a Samaritan.

The Samaritan represented the most despised, feared, and lowest class person imaginable to the religious people of Judea. But what the religious leaders refused to do, the Samaritan did!

He personally tended to the man's wounds, he placed him on a donkey, and he took him to a safe place where he could rest and recover. The Samaritan man also promised to return to check on the man's condition and pay all the costs related to his care and healing.

This parable is important because a Samaritan represented a mixed-race person who was looked down upon by the people of the day. However, Jesus chose a Samaritan which highlights the character of Christ. Love your neighbor!

The most obvious and perplexing way our world is in trouble is our separation, fear, and antagonism toward one another. We are divided by gender, race, class and other abuses. "Human beings have become progressively segregated... – a segregation matched by the steadily more competitive and even hostile relations between individuals and the larger human societies or states."[119] Divisiveness makes us choose sides. People, places, and things are branded as "other" and we become more loyal to that mentality than the people we serve. Yet, we are waiting for the world to change.

As a result, there is a deep and dividing tear in the fabric of our country. Once again, we find ourselves up against the Civil War mentality of the Confederacy. The old Pharaonic ideology of freedom for one somehow equals an attack on the life and liberty of the other. This notion could not be further from the truth and is based in fear. "It is the false and tragic notion that one particular group...is responsible for all of the progress. ... [and the] other group is totally depraved, innately impure, and innately inferior." [120] Many people of various backgrounds live in [this separate] America[121] - less than. Our division is our greatest tragedy.

Believe it or not, we are all connected. Not only are we one body of Christ as Christians, "we are tied together in language, music, culture, and prosperity."[122] John Donne says it like this, "no man is an island entire of itself."[123] We are all connected. Nothing demonstrates our connectedness more than the 2019-2021 COVID pandemic and its global effects. We seem like we are worlds apart, but the coronavirus found its way around the world. It hit home for my family for the first time in March of 2020.

My sister, Stacey, became sick on March 25, 2020. She immediately went to her physician who diagnosed her with strep throat. A week later, Stacey was admitted into the hospital with fluid in her lungs. It turns out she had contracted the Coronavirus from her place of employment. The Office Manager where Stacey worked refused to supply staff members with the proper protective equipment.

In the hospital, Stacey required oxygen but not a ventilator, so she was discharged with 'a little' fluid in her lungs without an oxygen tank. The next day, she was transported by ambulance to another hospital with breathing levels in the 70's due to the "little fluid" in her lungs. I called my sister who whispered and whimpered into the phone, "I am going to die." I encouraged her not to cry because it was stealing her last few breaths. I, then, called every prayer warrior I knew. We interceded for my sister.

Stacey had to fight for her life and proper healthcare as the hospital sought to release her again – with fluid in her lungs and without an oxygen tank. I recall her telling me how the doctor made her get out of bed and stand for a specified amount of time. The doctor also asked her to do a ridiculous breathing exercise to prove that she needed an in-home oxygen tank.

Stacey is fully insured so that was not the issue. Stacey endured two additional hospital stays for health problems as well as multiple trips to the pulmonologist and cardiologist. She was also prescribed a beta-blocker that would have killed her due to her low blood pressure. Stacey knew not to take the prescription as she is also a nurse. Prayer and being a nurse saved my sister's life. As an aside, one must wonder why Stacey was treated so poorly while fighting for her life.

As of March 16, 2021, over 120 million people globally had contracted the coronavirus with over 2.6 million losing their lives according to the World Health Organization.[124] America is responsible for 29.6+ million of the confirmed cases globally resulting in more than 530,000 deaths[125] and a startling number of the dead are African Americans and other minority groups.

Co-morbidities were a factor, however, there is mounting evidence that black Americans are disadvantaged in terms of access to diagnostic testing and treatment for the disease.[126] All the talk surrounding pre-existing conditions obscured a hidden truth: race is not what is making Black people more vulnerable to those illnesses, or to COVID-19. Racism is.[127] Scientists have long debunked the genetic difference between different races. Race is not biology. Race is a social construct. What is different is how we treat each other, which has a dramatic impact on access to care, fresh food, and exposure to dangerous environments.[128]

If you promote genetics as the problem, empathy is absolved. When empathy disappears policies to address and bridge disparities also disappear.[129]

Also, housing discrimination relegates BIPOC (Black Indigenous People of Color) "to inferior houses with mold and pest infestations such as mites, bed bugs, roaches, and rodents. BIPOC are far more likely to live in overcrowded housing. Therefore, there are no safe ways to shelter in place." [130]"Additionally, minorities are exposed more because they must leave the home for work and are less likely to have adequate personal protective equipment. The New York Times reviewed figures from the city's health department and found that when death rates are ranked by zip code, eight of the top 10 have majority Black or Latino populations."[131]

A growing body of evidence suggests that a person's zip code holds the most information about how long they will live. One's zip code directly affects health outcomes – from exposure to air pollution and toxins to accessibility of healthy food, green space, and medical care.[132]

"A government report in the UK[133] found 'historic racism and poorer experiences of healthcare or at work' put people of color at a higher risk of dying from the coronavirus."134 It cannot be that Black people globally are unhealthy. That is a prevarication. The housing, healthcare, and economic systems globally are unhealthy.

Perhaps our divisiveness prevented 'us' proverbially from helping our neighbor and crying with China before the global spread. What happens in China matters in Europe, America and beyond. To create a lasting change, we must connect in such a way it shifts the world.

If we hope to begin to heal the division, we must start by accepting people as they are. Acceptance cannot be one-dimensional or superficial. One of the absolute best things we can ever do for another person is listen to them, value their voice, and invite them to the table. This spirit is contagious and powerful. It affirms a foundational principle; that all of us have equal value as children of God.

Let me say, when we listen, we should not listen to discredit, disqualify, or compare experiences. We must listen to understand.

We can start by taking steps to diversify our social circle and get to know a different group of people. Interactions with different groups of people fosters understanding and better relations. You will be less likely to buy-in to universal stereotypes or biases. You may be able to guide another human being through the most difficult stages of their life.

When I began presenting, *I'm Perfectly Different*, I would give the same presentation to every audience. I quickly learned these presentations were ineffective. My audience was not a one size fits all. My presentations needed to be meaningful and gain depth. I had to ask questions and get to know more about the audience. I could walk into a group of six-year-olds and ask, "what is your favorite tv show?" and hear *Doc McStuffins, Sofia the First, Teen Titans GO,* and *Spiderman.* I asked a different group of six-year-olds the same question and hear White Collar, The Have and the Have Nots, and Scandal. I would have never guessed it but my presentation would require a different approach.

I also could not be afraid to be vulnerable. The same goes for our connectedness. Our connection needs to be deep, intentional, and indefinite. The deeper we get, the deeper we get.

This is not always easy even for Christians. It is uncomfortable to say the least. Some Christians choose Christ until the flesh becomes uncomfortable. Then we revert to old ways of thinking, doing, and being. Meanwhile, back in our comfort zone, we bump up against our unfiltered fleshiness or the tendency to operate out of our own understanding. We become lost to ourselves and essentially on our own. But we are dually connected.

Authentic compassion is another way beyond barriers. When we lose a compassionate connection with one another, people will make decisions to fulfill their own needs. Once this happens, we become powerless to intervene in times of trouble.

I have repeatedly seen people transform conflicted families and communities by utilizing compassion. This "movement of grace toward generosity doesn't come like a thunder bolt or an instant flash of spiritual insight, it comes as we practice the acts of grace. It becomes a habit like brushing your teeth and putting on deodorant, and it begins with a simple daily prayer, 'Help me not to be such a jerk today.'" [135]

Change cannot happen without unity on the most basic level which is humanity. Christ chose humanity. We cannot profess Christianity and not choose all of humanity. By treating human beings like human beings, we can change the world. This requires a shift in perspective from 'just me' to 'all of us.' We are all connected, and our differences should not cause division.

Being of the flesh, for the Apostle Paul, signifies living in rivalry and disunity within ourselves and this self-conflict spills over into other areas of our lives. Like Paul, we want all of God's people to grow and receive the fullness of God. Paul knew that the real measure of spiritual maturity was unity. To choose Christ means choosing community. Upholding unity during adversity is one of the most powerful ways we reveal the reality of what Jesus accomplished on the cross.[136]

"It takes a village" is a common idiom used to convey a sense of responsibility for one another. *I Heard the Owl Call My Name* – gives a great account of the village. *I Heard the Owl Call My Name* is a story of a priest who is assigned to lead a church at a remote village. The village is in disarray and transformation of the people did not come easily. However, a priestly revelation was formed during the transformation. As soon as you enter the village, you become a part of the village. The Village is You. [137]

Everyone has a responsibility to one another. It takes a village to make a difference. We are the village, and we are accountable to and for each other. Everything is associated with the village – cleanliness of your neighborhood, building maintenance, educational opportunities, social justice, government and so on. Caring for people where we are will change the world.

"The Revolution Will Not Be Televised" was a poem and song by Gil Scott-Heron. It was the B-side to Scott-Heron's first single, *"Home Is Where the Hatred Is"* but it came to over-shadow the A-side recording. The p oem h ighlights c omplacency, media, and capitalism as the antithesis of change. The poem further conveys that true change will not be resolved by the media or the rich who controls the narrative. The revolution begins with you in the community or using your platform to effect change.

Furthermore, large sections of the Bible tell us about God's involvement in sending people of faith where He wants them to be. God called Abram, later known as Abraham, to leave his home and journey to a place that God would show him. Give prayerful consideration to where God wants you to be planted.

I am where I am because I am called to be here. I could no longer wait for someone else to care for the broken. I must do my part and it begins in my community. Believe it or not, there are people counting on me remaining passive.

In the letter from the Birmingham jail, Dr. Martin Luther King Jr. latched onto a concept that I want us all to be aware of as we move forward. "We are... tied to a single garment of destiny. What affects one directly, affects all indirectly. (Therefore,) I can never be what I ought to be until you are what you ought to be. You can never be what you ought to be until I am what I ought to be."[138] Dr. King never lost sight of our **connectedness**...our connectedness to the spirit and to each other. Saints of God, we are all connected, and we all need each other.

Chapter 9

Finish the Race: We Shall Overcome

"...Run in such a way as to get the prize. Everyone
who competes in the games goes into strict training.
They do it to get a crown that will not last, but we do
it to get a crown that will last forever. Therefore I do
not run like someone running aimlessly."

1 Corinthians 9:24b-26a

There is a barrage of overarching conditions and narratives that contributes to your race in life. For instance, under resourced communities conditions and narratives are dictated by decision makers and outside forces. Much of these narratives greatly affects the quality of the race or life's journey.

John Henry is the name given to the hero of a Post-Civil War African American folk legend. Many people have sung about the plight of John the steel-driver. The story of John Henry focused on his race against the machine. You see, John's job was to hammer explosive holes in rocks using a steel drill when constructing railroad tunnels. Can you imagine how hard of a job that would be? Driving a steel peg into solid rock using a sledgehammer? A job like that requires an enormous amount of strength and wears on the body. Life for John was already hard before the race. As legend have it, John Henry raced against a steam-powered machine to prove himself. John Henry won the race but, sadly, John's heart gave out and John died.

John Henry has so many relatable undertones for people who are fighting against "the machine." The machine is a high-powered force with an infinite reach. The machine plows through objects, burying it beneath the ramble with ease. The ballad highlights inequity in labor and the race. It is believed that John Henry symbolized "foredoomed struggle [as well as the] tragic subjugation…and defiance of oppression."[139]

In *Finish the Race*, I am encouraging people to overcome obstacles. This race requires fortitude and perseverance. This race, however, is not a race to prove oneself worthy of the "machine." This race is to finish the good work God started in you. In this race, you are freeing yourself from the machine.

Therefore, since we are **surrounded by such a great cloud of witnesses,** let us throw off everything that hinders and the sin that so easily entangles. And let us run with perseverance the race marked out for us, **fixing our eyes on Jesus, the pioneer and perfecter of faith.** For the joy set before him he endured the cross, scorning its shame, and sat down at the right hand of the throne of God. Consider him who endured such opposition from sinners, so that you will not grow weary and lose heart. (Hebrews 12:1-3 NIV)

The only sure way to lose this race is to quit.

Gal 5:7-8, 10b is the premise of *Finish the Race*. Gal 5:7-8, 10b the English Standard Version says, "You were running well. Who hindered you from obeying the truth? This persuasion is not from him who calls you. ...the one who is troubling you will bear the penalty, whoever he is."

I love Galatians 5 because Paul is speaking to the people using the struggle between freedom and bondage as his metaphor. Paul makes it clear that freedom is given by God. God given freedom cannot be taken away by man. God-given freedom is liberation from sin. It is also liberation from anything that seeks to keep you from living into the purpose and plan of God. The literal word and the usage of freedom in the Greek 'eleutheria' means "liberty especially (in the sense of) freedom from slavery."[140] The Apostle Paul is directly addressing the end of slavery in every sense of the word. Therefore, it is not surprising that the Apostle Paul uses the imagery of running i.e., moving in the right direction. He then asks who cut in to stop you?

Have you ever been running, and someone cut you off? Ouch! The impact is more severe because of the momentum. Therefore, I am using Galatians 5:7-8, 10b to juxtapose freedom and running into life's biggest challenges.

Galatians 5:7-8, 10b is the precursor for overcoming life's mountains instead of becoming paralyzed by them and living in their shadow. My testimony of my ups and downs are chronicled throughout the book. I allowed feelings of shame and/or regret to shape my actions. Eckhart Tolle, author of the *Power of Now*, believes we create and maintain problems because they give us a sense of identity. Some of us are stuck in a mindset, traumatized by an event, living empty, buried alive. You cannot move forward. Past hurts provide present excuses for resisting life's changes, shifts and transformations.

In the autobiographical movie, *Antwone Fisher*, Antwone told his story as a troubled naval officer who suffered severe emotional trauma. Antwone's buried traumas to include mental, physical, and sexual abuse caused him to have violent outbursts which required him to see a psychiatrist. Antwone's escape from a life of further decay and despair came at the hands of a Naval officer who was plagued with his own traumas. This is a familiar story for many of us. Antwone allowed his traumas to define him. It stifled his life and perhaps the lives of those around him.

Each of us has experiences in our past that may be so painful that we get stuck in those moments and we end up carrying the pain with us. The burden of being stuck in the pain becomes a barrier separating us from ourselves and others. The experiences may involve family members, lovers, or confidantes which creates fragmented family ties because of unresolved pain and conflict.

Antwone reads a poem about this experience that says in part, "Who will cry for the little boy, lost and all alone? Who will cry for the little boy, abandoned without his own?" [141]

The Naval officer was willing to cry with Antwone outside of his professional position. This poem is indictive of someone who is asking for support to ease the hurting. However, the man was broken himself.

No one is waiting on a perfect person to help them. They are waiting for a person who is willing to listen and help even in their own brokenness. Are you willing to offer this type of support to your neighbor? Are you able to receive this type of support from your neighbor? Through helping Antwone heal, the navy officer found healing.

So, let me ask again. What is hindering you from living freely? Anything that prevents you from living freely is not from or of God. *Finish the Race* is the final message in this book.

Finish the Race is a part two of *I'm Perfectly Different* so to speak. *Finish the Race* creates a space for you to identify your hindrances, uncover the core causes, and takes a deeper dive into recognizing the root causes of emotional issues. Finish the Race hopes to demonstrate that you are bigger, better, and more powerful than your issues. I help individuals identify barriers and its' effects through a game called Red Rover.

Red Rover is a game where a team or two lock hands on either side of a room. One team calls out a player or players by saying "red rover, red rover, the player(s) wearing red may come over." The player(s) wearing red then runs with the goal of breaking the chain of the other team. If you fail to break the chain, you join the chain that prevents others from passing. After the game, I explain to the room that if we do not deal with the "thing" that is stopping us from running our race, it may become a barrier for someone else. Life's hinderances do not hinder only you. They hinder those cloud of witnesses running with you and behind you.

On every award show or acceptance speech we hear, "If it was not for those that came before me, I would not be here." Imagine all of the people who quit and its' effect on the people behind them. Your destiny may be tied to someone you do not know. We must fight against anything that hinders you from living freely into becoming who God created you to be.

It took some time for me to connect to what was stopping me from moving forward. For me, I had an issue with feeling uneducated. I would equate every mistake with stupidity. I have learned that stupidity is relative but that is a topic for another day.

My experience made me feel inferior, stupid, and less than others. I developed a fear of looking dim-witted publicly, so I stopped speaking up. I did not challenge statements and actions I did not agree with. This insecurity stopped me from running.

My obstacle was tied to my complexion. It had indoctrinated me. I was conditioned to feel inadequate. Therefore, when I made mistakes, I attributed it to being inferior opposed to a simple mistake. I went to a therapist to talk about the effects of my inferiority complex and my brother's suicide but repressed feelings from my grandmother surfaced.

I had no idea my grandmother's words about my family's complexion broke my spirit at an early age. Her words also contributed to my feelings of inferiority. This is the work of racism and racism's cousin colorism. Racism done well enslaves the mind of the elders. Hatred is passed down to the children and the work of oppression is done. Generations of people are hindered as a result. This is how the afflicted stay afflicted or stop running. This damage had the propensity to stifle my life permanently. If I allowed my insecurity to stop me, I would not be able to encourage countless people to keep running. My limitations could have limited someone else's worldview.

I have since embraced mistakes. Mistakes are a part of the learning process. I do not know everything and that is fine. I can learn as I grow. I will make mistakes, but I will change how I reacted to them. OOPS!

I do not fear looking inferior. Now, no one can keep me from talking. If I do not understand things as quickly as others, it is okay. If I need to ask more questions, I will boldly gain clarity. Fear becomes less when there is less to fear. I know who I am. The same is true for you. You do not have to be afraid of your feelings. Refocus and recognize the root of the feeling. A huge part of my adult life has been freeing myself while freeing others. I implore you to do the same.

Finish the race! Move forward by continually facing the truth about what is hindering you. You are not the mistake you made. It may seem like the world shows you no penance for your mistakes but that is not who you are.

By the way, Moses was a murderer before he became one of the greatest leaders in Christian history. Shift your perspective and stop trying to figure out who you are meant to be. God already told you.

You are fearfully and wonderfully made; your works are wonderful; I know that full well. (Psalm 139:14 NIV) What is stopping you from being all that God said you are?

As you take some time to reflect on what is stopping you, I would like to offer the matrix I utilize to help me figure out what is stopping me. It is an acronym for race. The acronym R.A.C.E. is what also helps me when I feel momentarily stifled. I hope it helps you as well.

R.A.C.E.

Recognize what it is that is stopping you

Acknowledge its effect on you and why

Change your response to the obstacle

Eliminate it as an obstacle

Continue to run!

If I use my scenario from above.

Recognize: I recognized that I had a problem feeling inferior. My issue with inferiority bleed into all areas of my life.

Acknowledge: It stopped me from speaking up and fully participating in every area of my life. It was attributed to my complexion.

Change: I realized that it is okay to make mistakes and mistakes does not mean I am inferior. Nothing makes me inferior to anyone.

Eliminate: I am no longer afraid to speak up because I know I am not less than anyone else. I also overcame the desire to shrink back.

R.A.C.E. is not a one-time occurrence. You may have to revisit a scenario more than once. Breaking free from anything that hinders you must be identified and rethought as many times as you need to in order to move forward. Also, trust that the Lord is racing with you.

I was on my way to the office. I was thinking about this book. Suddenly, a wave of insecurities washed over me. I took a deep breath and started to R.A.C.E. I was speaking it out loud to the Lord as I was driving. In the distance, I saw a billboard with the bold blue words, "Have No Fear..." Now, I have traveled the same roads for nearly three years. I never saw this sign. I knew God was speaking to me directly. I was instantly reassured and changed the way I was thinking. I am moving forward – overcoming obstacles in my heart and mind.

We are overcomers. Anything we want to do we can do. Trust yourself, believe in yourself and keep going! Finish the R.A.C.E. – Recognize, Acknowledge, Change, Eliminate it as a barrier. Also, if you find yourself needing help overcoming your own biases, please feel free to R.A.C.E.

Resist the urge to judge or stereotype people who are different from you.

Acknowledge the person you are communicating with. Be present in the moment.

Do not listen **comparatively** which is listening to discredit, disqualify, or compare experiences. Listen with a spirit of understanding someone else's struggles.

Embrace people fully for who they are.

Finish the R.A.C.E. – **R**esist, **A**cknowledge, (no) **C**omparative listening, **E**mbrace.

Do not let anything hold you back. If you must tell your story to a therapist, pastor, or trusted confidant to become more self-aware, do it. There are people behind you and at the finish line waiting for you. Keep going and lead others into the Promised Land. The place of abundance.

You have heard me teach things that have been confirmed by many reliable witnesses. Now teach these truths to other trustworthy people who will be able to pass them on to others. 2 Timothy 2:2 New Living Translation (NLT)

There is a way out.

By the way, in Biblical Greek, e'basis is the word for way. It is interesting because it is defined as coming out from **and moving toward a** new destination by removing all that hinders you. I love e'basis' use in 1 Corinthians 10:13 (God) "will also provide a way out..." because way means the Lord's outcome. "Trust in the Lord with all your heart; do not depend on your own understanding. Seek his will in all you do, and he will show you which path to take." (Proverbs 3:5-6 NLT) Trust God and move forward in faith. I will see you at the finish line.

Footnotes by Chapter

Chapter 2

1   Poverty typically is measured by the purchasing power of a household. Purchasing power has a strong correlation to most other living condition indices and is therefore used as a main indicator of poverty. Poverty is used to indicate the socioeconomic class of a population. http://money.cnn.com/2011/09/13/news/economy/poverty_rate_income/index.htm

2   Abhijit V. Banerjee ve Esther Duflo, Poor Economics: A Radical Rethinking of the Way to Fight Global Poverty (2012): 335.

3   United Nations Statement of commitment for action to eradicate poverty adopted by administrative committee on coordination. Retrieved from https://www.un.org/press/en/1998/19980520.eco5759.html, (1998).

4   The Cost of Poverty: The Perpetuating Cycle of Concentrated Poverty in New Jersey Cities, (2016): 5.

5   Darrick Hamilton, "Race, Wealth and Intergenerational Poverty," The American Prospect 20 (August 2009): 21.

6   Shaun Donovan, Arne Duncan and Kathleen Sebelius, "Fighting poverty through community development", (2012): 109.

7   J. Brooks-Gunn & G. J. Duncan, The effects of poverty on children. (1997): 57.

8   Howard Thurman. Jesus and the Disinherited, (1976): 55.

9   Howard Thurman, Jesus and the Disinherited, (1976): 55

10   Shaun Donovan, Arne Duncan and Kathleen Sebelius, "Fighting poverty through community development." Investing in What Works for American's communities: Essays on People, Place, and Purpose, edited by Nancy O Andrews, David J Erickson, Ian J Galloway, and Ellen S Seidman (2012): 108.

11   Poverty Guidelines | ASPE (hhs.gov)

12   Income and Poverty in the United States: 2019 (census.gov) (Table B-1)

13   Wendy Nadel & Shirley Sagawa, America's Forgotten Children: Child Poverty in Rural America, (2002): 12.

14   Emily Badger, "More and more Americans are living with the 'double burden' of concentrated poverty", The Washington Post,

     https://www.washingtonpost.com/news/wonk/wp/2014/08/01/

     moreandmoreamericans-are-living-with thedouble-burden-of-

     concentrated-poverty, August 1, 2014.

15   The Cost of Poverty, (2016): 15.

16   Cost of poverty, (2016): 9-10.

17   https://www.census.gov/data/tables/time-series/demo/income-po-verty/historical-poverty-thresholds.html

18   Julio de Santa Ana, Good news to the poor: the challenge of the poor in the history of the church, (1979): 1.

19   Reinhold Niebhur, Moral Man Immoral Society, (1960): 9,

20   Julio de Santa Ana, 1.

21   Susan R. Holman, The Hungry Are Dying: Beggars and Bishops in Roman Cappadocia, (2001), 5.

22 Holman, 6.

23 Holman, 5.

24 Holman, 5.

25 Holman, 6.

26 Holman, 6.

27 Ibid.

28 Julio de Santa Ana, (1979), 1.

29 Justo L. González, Faith and wealth: A History of Early Christian Ideas on the Origin, Significance, and Use of Money, (1990), 133.

30 González, 134.

31 Howard Thurman, 17.

32 Reinhold Niebuhr, Moral Man Immoral Society, (1960) :17-18

33 Howard Thurman, Jesus and the Disinherited, 74.

34 Niebuhr, Moral Man Immoral Society, (1960): 91.

35 Gregory Mantsios and Paula S. Rothenberg. Race, Class and Gender in the United States. (2004): 203.

36 Mantsios, 202.

37 Mantsios, 194.

38 George Carlin, Life is Worth Losing, HBO Special, (2005).

39 Mantsios, 194.

40 Domhoff, 9.

41 Niebuhr, 9.

42 Niebuhr, 117-118.

43 Niebuhr, 118

44 Wells Fargo CEO's comments about diverse talent anger some emp-

loyees, https://www.cnbc.com/2020/09/22/wells-fargo-ceo-ruffles-feathers-with-comments-about-diverse-talent.html, Assessed April 17, 2021.

45   ibid., https://www.nbcnews.com/news/nbcblk/wells-fargo-ceo-ruffles-feathers-comments-about-diverse-talent-n1240739, Assessed April 17, 2021.

46   Niebuhr, 113.

47   Thurman, 20.

48   Niebuhr, Moral Man Immoral Society, 1.

Chapter 3

49   Small Towns BIG IDEAS: Case Studies in Small Town Community Economic Development, (2008): 157. https://www.sog.unc.edu/sites/www.sog.unc.edu/files/stbi_final.pdf

50   Municipal Land Use Law: New Jersey Statutes Annotated Historic Preservation Related Sections,

https://www.nj.gov/dep/hpo/3preserve/mlul_02_2017.pdf, February 2017.

51   How the Municipal Land Use Law and Municipal Master Plan shape the Municipal Zoning Ordinance, MLUL & Master Plan Shape the Zoning Ordinance.pdf (rutgers.edu), 1

52   Ibid.

53   Ibid.

54   Angela Fields, "Master Plan: more bad news for the Urban Poor", Associated Baptist Press, (2011).

55   Negro invasion is promoting negative imagery, ideology, and stereotypes to develop a fear or hatred of Black people.

56   Richard Rothstein, The Color of Law, (2017): 12

57   Rothstein, 12.

58   Shaun Donovan, Arne Duncan and Kathleen Sebelius, 116.

59   Shaun Donovan, Arne Duncan and Kathleen Sebelius, 116.

60   Shaun Donovan, Arne Duncan and Kathleen Sebelius, 117.

61   Howard Thurman, 39,44.

62   Dudley Poston and Rogelio Sáenz, "The US white majority will soon disappear forever", The Chicago Reporter. 2019.

63   Terence Fretheim, "Interpretation, A Bible commentary for teaching and preaching: Exodus," John Knox Press, (1991), 84-85.

64   Angela Fields, Poverty in Paradise, Christian Ethics Today, Spring 2013, 25.

65   Terence Fretheim, 84.

66   Angela Fields, 25

67   Daniel Goleman, Emotional intelligence: Why it Can Matter more than IQ, Bantam Books, (2005) :156.

68   Martin L. King Jr., Stride towards Freedom, HarperSanFrancisco, (1958): 93.

69   King Jr., Stride towards Freedom, 37.

70   Niebuhr, 121

71   Goleman, 156-157.

72   Bailey, Amy Kate, and Karen A. Snedker. "Practicing What They Preach? Lynching and Religion in the American South, 1890–1929." American Journal of Sociology, vol. 117, no. 3, 2011, pp. 844–887. JSTOR, www.jstor.org/stable/10.1086/661985. Accessed 8 Apr. 2021.

73 Alan Jones, Soul Making: The Desert Way of Spirituality, HarperSan-Francisco (1985), 159-162.

74 Martin L. King Jr., Why we can't wait, (Signet Classics, 1963), 12.

75 https://www.history.com/news/5-things-you-may-not-know-about-lincoln-slavery-and-emancipation

76 https://www.history.com/news/5-things-you-may-not-know-about-lincoln-slavery-and-emancipation

77 Bryan Stevenson, TED Talk, We need to talk about an Injustice, June 7, 2021.

78 Gabrielle Union, Pricing out of Racism, Interview with The Root, November 2017.

79 https://www.harpersbazaar.com/culture/features/a18822/gabrielle-union-interview/

80 https://www.washingtonpost.com/graphics/2020/opinions/systemic-racism-police-evidence-criminal-justice-system/ (Radley Balko) June 10, 2020

81 https://www.history.com/topics/early-20th-century-us/jim-crow-laws

82 Radley Balko

83 Radley Balko

84 Balko, https://www.washingtonpost.com/graphics/2020/opinions/systemic-racism-police-evidence-criminal-justice-system/, June 10, 2020

85 The Devil's Advocate. Directed by Taylor Hackford. Perfor. by Keanu Reeves, Al Pacino, and Charlize Theron. Warner Bros Pictures. 1997. Film.

86 The Devil's Advocate.

87 Reinhold Niebuhr, 21.

88   I am stating the above with the understanding that certain activities are criminalized like loitering to force poor people and people of color into the criminal justice system.

Chapter 4

89   Dr. Martin Luther King Jr., Stride toward Freedom, 194.

90   Howard Thurman, 94.

Chapter 5

91   Thurman, 86.

92   "The emotional core of love: the centrality of emotion in Christian psychology and ethics." The Free Library. 2012 CAPS International (Christian Association for Psychological Studies) 22 Jun. 2021

93   Daniel Goleman, 289.

94   Goleman, 102.

95   Goleman, 99.

96   King, Jr., 194.

97   Anne Lamont, Help, Thanks, Wow, Riverhead Books, (2012): 86.

98   Goleman, 34.

99   Sophia is the Greek word for wisdom

Chapter 6

100 James Orr, M.A., D.D. General Editor. "Entry for 'SHEPHERD'". "International Standard Bible Encyclopedia". 1915.

101 Easton, Matthew George. "Entry for Shepherd". "Easton's Bible Dictionary" Third Edition, published by Thomas Nelson, 1897.

102 The New Smith's Bible Dictionary

103 Angela Fields, Poverty in Paradise, Christian Ethics Today. The Christian Ethics Foundation. Spring 2013: Issue 89, Pages 24-25.

104 Angela Fields, 25

105 Fields, 25

106 S. A. McLeod, Maslow's Hierarchy of needs. Simply Psychology, (2020, March 20). https://www.simplypsychology.org/maslow.html

107 S. A. McLeod, Maslow's Hierarchy of needs. Simply Psychology, (2020, March 20). https://www.simplypsychology.org/maslow.html

108 McLeod, https://www.simplypsychology.org/maslow.html

109 McLeod.

110 https://www.dictionary.com/browse/stockholm-syndrome

111 Gary Gunderson, Deeply Woven Roots, Fortress Press (1997): 106, 100, 99 respectively.

Chapter 7

112 Leonard, Pitts Jr., Leadership requires ability to walk in someone else's shoes, https://www.dispatch.com/article/20130321/OPINION/303219769, March 2013, originally accessed through the Miami Herald 2013.

113 Robert Linthicum, Transforming Power: Biblical Strategies for Making a Difference in Your Community, (2003): 81.

114 Robert Linthicum, 82

115 Marianne Williamson, A Return to Love: Reflections on the Principles of "A Course in Miracles, (1992), HarperOne.

116 Charles H. Spurgeon, Walk humbly with thy God – Micah 6:8. Sermon presented at the Metropolitan Tabernacle, Newington, London, (1889, August).

117 Ibid, Charles Spurgeon.

Chapter 8

118 Anne Lamont, 62.

119 Fred Dallmayr, Integral Pluralism: Beyond Culture Wars, University of Press of Kentucky, (2010):

1.

120 Martin L King Jr., The Other America, Speech delivered at Stanford University, 14 April 1967.

121 King Jr., The Other America

122 King Jr., The Other America

123 King Jr., The Other America

124 https://www.who.int/emergencies/diseases/novel-coronavirus-2019

125 Coronavirus in the US: Latest Map and Case Count https://www.nytimes.com/interactive/2020/us/coronavirus-us-cases.html

126 Ed Pilkington, Black Americans dying of Covid-19 at three times the rate of white people, The guardian May 20, 2020.

127 Hilary Brueck and Canela Lopez, The Racial gap in coronavirus deaths is driven by racism, The business insider, Jun 19, 2020.

128 Hilary Brueck and Canela Lopez

129 Hilary Brueck and Canela Lopez

130 Hilary Brueck and Canela Lopez

131 Ed Pilkington, Black Americans dying of Covid-19 at three times the rate of white people, The guardian May 20, 2020.

132 Jamie Ducharme & Elijah Wolfson, Your ZIP Code Might Determine How Long You Live—and the Difference Could Be Decades, Time, JUNE 17, 2019.

133 Public Health England (PHE) as per the BBC

134 Hilary Brueck and Canela Lopez, The Racial gap in coronavirus deaths is driven by racism, The business insider, Jun 19, 2020.

135 Anne Lamont excerpt from Help, Thanks, Wow.

136 Brenda Salter McNeil. A Credible Witness: Reflections on Power, Evangelism and Race, InterVarsity Press Publication, (2008).

137 Margaret Craven, I Heard the Owl Call my Name, Totem, (1976).

138 Martin L King Jr., Why We Can't Wait, Signet Classics, 1963: 87.

Chapter 9

139 John Henry: Folk Hero, https://www.britannica.com/topic/John-Henry-folk-hero

140 Strong Concordance

141 Antwone Fisher, Who Will Cry for the Boy?, Harper Collins, (2003):1.

Bibliography

Badger, Emily. *More and more Americans are living with the 'double burden' of concentrated poverty.* The Washington Post, August 1, 2014.

Bailey, Amy Kate, and Karen A. Snedker. *Practicing What They Preach? Lynching and Religion in the American South, 1890–1929.* American Journal of Sociology, vol. 117, no. 3, 2011, pp. 844–887. JSTOR, www.jstor.org/stable/10.1086/661985. Accessed April 8 2021.

Balko, Radley. *There's overwhelming evidence that the criminal justice system is racist. Here's the proof.* https://www.washingtonpost.com/graphics/2020/opinions/systemic-racism-police-evidence criminal-justice-system/, June 10, 2020, Assessed November 20, 2020.

Banerjee, Abhijit V. and Esther Duflo. *Poor Economics: A Radical Rethinking of the Way to Fight Global Poverty.* Public Affairs, 2012.

Brooks-Gunn, Jeanne, and Greg J. Duncan. *The Effects of Poverty on Children.* The Future of Children, vol. 7, no. 2, 1997, pp. 55–71. JSTOR, www.jstor.org/stable/1602387.

Brueck, Hilary and Canela Lopez. *The Racial gap in coronavirus deaths is driven by racism.* The business insider, Jun 19, 2020.

Carlin, George. *Life is Worth Losing.* HBO Special, 2005.

Craven, Margaret. *I Heard the Owl Call my Name.* Totem, 1976.

Dallmayr, Fred. *Integral Pluralism: Beyond Culture Wars.* University of Press of Kentucky, 2010.

Domhoff, G. William. *Who Rules America? Power and Politics.* McGraw Hill, 2002.

Donovan, Shaun, Arne Duncan and Kathleen Sebelius, *"Fighting Poverty through Community Development." Investing in What Works for American's communities: Essays on People, Place, and Purpose,* edited by Nancy O Andrews, David J Erickson, Ian J Galloway and Ellen S Seidman, Federal Reserve Bank of San Francisco and Low-Income Investment Fund, 2012, 107-131.

Du Bois, W.E.B. *The Souls of Black Folk.* Dover Publications, Inc, 1994.

Ducharme, Jaime & Elijah Wolfson. *Your ZIP Code Might Determine How Long You Live—and the Difference Could Be Decades,* Time, June 17, 2019.

Easton, Matthew George. *Entry for Shepherd.* Easton's Bible Dictionary, Third Edition. Thomas Nelson, 1897.

Elliott, Matthew. "The emotional core of love: the centrality of emotion in Christian psychology and ethics." Journal of Psychology and Christianity, vol. 31, no. 2, 2012, p. 105+. Gale Academic OneFile, link.gale.com/apps/doc/A342175914/E?u=anon-33272361&sid=goo gleScholar&xid=523bcde6. Accessed 21 July 2021.

Fields, Angela. *Master Plan: more bad news for the Urban Poor.* Associated Baptist Press, 2011.

Fields, Angela. *Poverty in Paradise.* Christian Ethics Today. The Christian Ethics Foundation. Spring 2013: Issue 89. Print.

Fisher, Antwone. *Who Will Cry for the Boy?* (New York: Harper Collins, 2003).

Goleman, Daniel. *Emotional Intelligence: Why it Can Matter More Than IQ.* Bantam Books, 2005.

González, Justo L. *Faith and Wealth: A History of Early Christian Ideas on the Origin, Significance, and Use of Money.* Harper & Row Publishers, 1990.

Gunderson, Gary. *Deeply Woven Roots.* Fortress Press, 1997.

Hamilton, Darrick. *"Race, Wealth, and Intergenerational Poverty."* The American Prospect, August 14, 2009, 13-17.

Holman, Susan R. *The Hungry are Dying: Beggars and Bishops in Roman Cappadocia.* Oxford University Press, 2001.

Jones, Alan. *Soul Making: The Desert Way of Spirituality,* HarperSanFrancisco, 1989.

King Jr., Martin Luther. *Stride toward Freedom: The Montgomery Story.* HarperSanFrancisco, 1986.

King Jr., Martin Luther. *Why we can't wait.* Signet Classics, 1963.

King Jr. Martin L. *The Other America,* Speech delivered at Stanford University, 14 April 1967.

Lamont, Anne. *Help, Thanks, Wow.* Riverhead Books, 2012.

Lemmons. The New Smith's Bible Dictionary. Garden City NY: Doubleday & Co, 1979. Print.

Linthicum, Robert. *Transforming Power: Biblical Strategies for Making a Difference in Your Community.* IVP Books, 2003.

Mantsios, Gregory and Paula S. Rothenberg. "Class in America." *Race, Class and Gender in the United States.* Worth Publishers, 2004.

McLeod, S.A. *Maslow's Hierarchy of needs.* Simply Psychology, 20 March 2020. https://www.simplypsychology.org/maslow.html

McNeil, Brenda S. *A Credible Witness: Reflections on Power, Evangelism and Race,* InterVarsity Press Publication, 2008.

Nadel, Wendy and Shirley Sagawa. *America's Forgotten Children: Child Poverty in Rural America.* Distribution by ERIC Clearinghouse, 2002.

Niebuhr, Reinhold. *Moral Man and Immoral Society: A Study in Ethics and Politics.* Westminster John Knox Press, 1960.

Orr, James, M.A., D.D. General Editor. *Entry for 'SHEPHERD.* International

Standard Bible Encyclopedia, 1915.

Pilkington, Ed. *Black Americans dying of Covid-19 at three times the rate of white people.* The Guardian, May 20, 2020.

Pitts Jr. Leonard. *Leadership requires ability to walk in someone else's shoes.* https://www.dispatch.com/article/20130321/OPINION/303219769, March 2013, originally assessed through the Miami Herald 2013.

Poston, Dudley and Rogelio Sáenz. *The US white majority will soon disappear forever.* The Chicago Reporter. 2019.

Ramsey, Boniface. *Almsgiving in the Latin church: The Late Fourth and Early Fifth Centuries.* Theological Studies, 43, 1982, 226-259.

Rothstein, Richard. *The Color of Law: A Forgotten History of How our Government Segregated America.* Live Right Publishing Corporation, 2017.

Santa Ana, Julio de. *Good News to the Poor: The Challenge of the Poor in the History of the Church.* Orbis Books, 1979.

Spurgeon, C. H. *Walk humbly with thy God – Micah 6:8.* Sermon presented at the Metropolitan Tabernacle, Newington, CT. (1889, August).

Stevenson, Bryan. *We need to talk about an Injustice,* Ted Talk. Assessed on June 7, 2021.

Thurman, Howard. *Jesus and the Disinherited.* Beacon Press,1976.

The John S. Watson Institute for Public Policy of Thomas Edison State University in partnership with the New Jersey Urban Mayors Association. *The Cost of Poverty: The Perpetuating Cycle of Concentrated Poverty in New Jersey Cities.* 2016.

Union, Gabrielle Pricing out of Racism, Interview with The Root, November 2017.

https://www.harpersbazaar.com/culture/features/a18822/gabrielle-union-interview/

Wells Fargo CEO's comments about diverse talent anger some employees,
https://www.cnbc.com/2020/09/22/wells-fargo-ceo-ruffles-feathers-with-comments about-diverse-talent.html, Assessed April 17, 2021.

Williamson, Marianne. *A Return to Love: Reflections on the Principles of "A Course in Miracles.* HarperOne, 1992.

https://www.history.com/topics/early-20th-century-us/jim-crow-laws

Made in the USA
Las Vegas, NV
28 January 2022

42498188R00089